"*Mindful Motherhood* contains what so many other parenting books omit: the consoling information that each mother has the ability to know, deep within, how to care for her child. Mindful Motherhood is a gem."

—Christiane Northrup, MD, author of *Women's Bodies, Women's Wisdom*

"Wise, soothing, and helpful—this is really good stuff for new mothers."

— Jack Kornfield, author of *The Wise Heart*

"In *Mindful Motherhood*, you'll experience the wisdom of a mother, clinician, and researcher who outlines the accessible, practical steps to take to turn challenge into triumph during pregnancy and the parenting of young children. Read this book, give it as a baby shower present, carry it with you into the pediatrician's office— but most of all, take it in and savor its secrets for a richer life for yourself and your child."

—Daniel J. Siegel, MD, author of *Parenting from the Inside Out* and *The Mindful Brain*

"This book will inspire, guide, and reassure mothers in pregnancy and after childbirth. Nothing could be more important to our families, our children, and the future of the world. Dads will benefit, also."

—Paul Ekman, Ph.D., coauthor, with the Dalai Lama, of *Emotional Awareness*

"The connection between mother and baby is one of the most spiritual relationships we have."

—Baba Ram Dass, also known as Richard Alpert, author of *Remember, Be Here Now*

"This is a beautiful book—deeply moving, intensely practical, and filled with wisdom."

—Ruth A. Baer, Ph.D., professor of psychology at University of Kentucky

D0176353

"This is a welcome and needed book. These practical meditations for women may be a great help with prenatal and postnatal challenges. These essential psychological practices come from a woman who has earned the right to teach a classical path of human development through motherhood."

—Robert Bruce Newman, author of *Calm Birth and Calm Healing*

"Mindfulness, when extended from mother to child, weaves a blanket of grounded attunement sufficient for two. Cassandra Vieten's down-to-earth suggestions will help all newly enlarged families navigate this wonderful, but often disruptive milestone."

—Zindel V. Segal, Ph.D., C.Psych., Morgan Firestone Chair in Psychotherapy at the Centre for Addiction and Mental Health in Toronto, ON, Canada

"With wisdom, depth, and humility, *Mindful Motherhood* guides us through the miraculous and challenging path of becoming a mother. It weaves together scholarship, personal experience, and practical tools, helping us become the most loving, present and joyful parents we can be. As a scholar and mother, I found this book immensely valuable."

—Shauna Shapiro, coauthor, with Linda Carlson, of *The Art and Science of Mindfulness*

"Vieten writes with love and tenderness about the mindful mother and the importance of staying in the present. Regardless of the age of your child, you will never go wrong by acting as a teacher of love and patience."

—Jerry Jampolsky, MD, coauthor of *A Mini Course for Life*

mindful motherhood

Practical Tools for Staying Sane During Pregnancy and Your Child's First Year

cassandra vieten, ph.d.

Noetic Books, Institute of Noetic Sciences
New Harbinger Publications, Inc.

Publisher's Note

Distributed in Canada by Raincoast Books

A copublication of New Harbinger Publications and Noetics Books.

Copyright © 2009 by Cassandra Vieten
New Harbinger Publications, Inc.
5674 Shattuck Avenue
Oakland, CA 94609
www.newharbinger.com

"Silence," © 2005, from *Too Intimate for Words*, published by Integrative Arts, is reprinted with permission from John Astin.

"Come Rest," © 2009, is printed with permission from John Astin.

"The Guest House" is reprinted with permission from Coleman Barks. Originally published in *The Essential Rumi*, © 1997, translated by Coleman Barks, Harper Collins, page 109.

Cover design by Amy Shoup; Text design by Amy Shoup and Michele Waters-Kermes; Acquired by Catharine Sutker

---

Library of Congress Cataloging-in-Publication Data

Vieten, Cassandra.
 Mindful motherhood : practical tools for staying sane in pregnancy and your child's first year / Cassandra Vieten ; foreword by Sylvia Boorstein.
    p. cm.
Includes bibliographical references.
 ISBN-13: 978-1-57224-629-4 (pbk. : alk. paper)
 ISBN-10: 1-57224-629-4 (pbk. : alk. paper)
 1. Motherhood. I. Title.
HQ759.V533 2009
155.6'463--dc22

2009007133

FSC
Mixed Sources
Product group from well-managed
forests and other controlled sources

Cert no. SW-COC-002283
www.fsc.org
© 1996 Forest Stewardship Council

11   10   09

10   9   8   7   6   5   4   3   2   1   First printing

This book is dedicated to David and Indigo

and to my circle of fabulous moms

starting with my own, Billie, whose strength and wisdom are a source of
constant support, Ameae, whose grace and goodwill have kept me afloat
in ways she may not even realize, and to the mamas who support
and inspire me more each day:

Amy

Avvy

Elana

Jean

Jen

Jnana

Julia

Kim

Rachel

Vicky

&

Wendy

contents

Section 2
The Qualities of Mindful Motherhood

Section 3
Mindful Motherhood in Everyday Life

acknowledgments

this book was years in the making and is the product of many, many contributions.

First, thanks to Jean Doyle and Mary Gregory of the Bella Vista Foundation, who funded the development of and research on the Mindful Motherhood Program and the creation of this book and the accompanying website. Deep thanks also to Virginia Hubble, Julie Diamond, and everyone at the Mental Insight Foundation, who also generously contributed to this work.

Heartfelt thanks to Catharine Sutker, Jess Beebe, Carole Honeychurch, Amy Shoup, Matt McKay, and everyone at New Harbinger, and to Matthew Gilbert at Noetic Books, who all helped to shepherd this book to completion.

Warm appreciation to my colleague John Astin, who collaborated with me on the Mindful Motherhood Project and who has influenced me tremendously with his clear sight and warm heart.

Deep gratitude to Jnana Gowan, who developed the Mindful Motherhood Yoga Series and partnered with me to facilitate the Mindful Motherhood Program as it was developed.

Thanks to Suze Allen at Manuscript Mentor, who provided additional editing.

Thanks to Billie Rogers for more help with editing.

Thanks to all the people who worked on the Mindful Motherhood Project, including Amy Beddoe, Lisa Bialy, Raymond Buscemi, Mary Costello, Sharifa Karen Krongold, Sue Louiseau, Liz Miller, Daniel Rechtstaffen, Jessica Welborn, and Vicky Willey.

More gratitude to Warren Browner and California Pacific Medical Center's Research Institute, and the Institute of Noetic Sciences, both of which supported and hosted this project.

And finally, thanks to people who advised, consulted, or provided inspiration for the Mindful Motherhood Project, including Nancy Bardacke, Sylvia Boorstein, Sona Dimidjian, Elissa Epel, Rick Hanson, Jon Kabat-Zinn, Dacher Keltner, Kari Marble, Gayle Peterson, Ricki Pollycove, Marilyn Schlitz, Zindel Segal, and Phil Shaver.

foreword

when my first child, Michael, was born just over fifty years ago in Topeka, Kansas, I had two "baby books" to provide instructions and support: *The Common Sense Book of Baby and Child Care* (1957) by Dr. Benjamin Spock and *Mother and Child* by Dr. D. W. Winnicott (1957). I was living in a new city with my graduate-student husband. My mother lived a thousand miles away—a longer distance than a thousand miles is now with cell phones. I'd been an only child in a post-Depression era in which people had few children. The first diaper I changed in my whole life was the one I put on Michael when I dressed him to take him home from the hospital. And we used pins to fasten cloth diapers. "Be careful not to stick him," the nurse said to me as she watched me struggle a too-bunched-up cloth diaper onto Michael's less-than-six-pounds-altogether body.

I consulted my Dr. Spock book regularly for advice about what relieves colic, what varieties of color or consistency poop can be and still be within the limits of normal, or when to suspect that my baby had an ear infection. But I read the Winnicott book often, perhaps daily, to keep my courage intact. The book is now long out of print, having been incorporated into *The Child, the Family and The Outside World* (1992). I gave my copy away long ago, but the first passage, as I remember it, is something close to, "I don't know how to take care of your baby, because it is your baby and you are the baby's mother and you will know. You'll know *because* you are the baby's mother, and you are tied together by a natural bond of love. Mothers, for time immemorial, have known how to take care of their babies without advice books from other people." Perhaps not those exact words, but words just like those. I was more than encouraged. I was consoled. Even, perhaps especially, on difficult days. On days when I tried this or that in response to Michael's distress and nothing seemed to be effective and I'd be feeling, "Eeeeek!"—I'd think, "I'm his mother. I love him. We'll work this out."

How I wish I'd had *Mindful Motherhood* with me then. This superb presentation of basic techniques for steadying the mind, keeping it sane and buoyant and confident in the midst of pregnancy and new-baby care sounds to me like the reassurance of Winnicott—"You are the parent; you can do it because you love naturally"—and the wisdom of the Buddha—"You are not your thoughts, or your moods, that all pass; you are, in your essence, benevolence"—spoken in the idiom of a modern woman who is also a mother.

Had I had *Mindful Motherhood* with me fifty years ago, I would have thought of Cassi Vieten as my friend.

—Sylvia Boorstein

introduction: riding the waves of motherhood

pregnancy, childbirth, and early motherhood can be both particularly challenging and incredibly rewarding. The rapid changes in your body, your lifestyle, your relationships, your work, even your very identity can call for a certain agility, like running an obstacle course or training for a marathon. Mindful motherhood, as a set of skills, can help prepare you to meet these challenges in ways that you can apply in your everyday life. Mindful motherhood, as a way of being, is a heartfelt way to gently meet the thoughts, feelings, and situations you will be faced with as a pregnant woman and new mom.

what is mindful motherhood?

First, I want you to know that being mindful is not yet another goal you must achieve to be a good mom. It's not about becoming a perfect Zen mama who stays calm, cool, and collected in the face of anything that comes; uses only organic baby foods, clothing, *and* linens; stays on a career path while also being available to her family; and stays fit and trim all the while. The last thing I want to do with this book is put another giant task on your list of "things I must do to be a good mom." Mindful motherhood is not about becoming someone other than who you already are.

Mindful motherhood, simply put, is being present, in your body, and connected with your baby no matter what is happening. It's being aware of your experience from moment to moment, as it is happening, without pushing it away, trying to make it stay, or judging it as bad or good. It is meeting each situation as it is, and over time, more and more often, approaching whatever is happening with curiosity and compassion.

Mindful motherhood is a way of approaching all of the experiences you'll encounter as a mom with open eyes and an open heart. Whether those experiences are internal, like thoughts, feelings, or body sensations; or external, like relationships, workplace situations, or the situations in your environment, mindful motherhood is a way of simply *being with* whatever is happening, no matter what it is. While it may be simple, for most of us, it's not easy.

Take this example. It's 3 a.m. and the baby is crying—screaming, actually. This is the fourth night you've been up with the baby more than three times in the middle of the night, and you haven't had more than two hours of continuous sleep in a few days. Naturally, you are getting a bit raw, overwhelmed, and angry.

Your train of thought might be something along these lines: "Why can't I get this baby to sleep? All the babies in my mothers' group are sleeping through the night. What is wrong with me?" Or, "What's wrong with my baby? Maybe she has colic. Oh crap, that means it's going to be like this every night for six months—I won't be able to take it! Should I give her a bottle? The book says no bottle at night because that will just keep her waking up forever…And why isn't John coming in here to help? I can't believe he has the nerve to stay in bed and pretend he didn't hear this. Jeez, why is it so cold in here? Our heater never works right. For God's sake, please stop screaming…" Your body gets tense, tears come to your eyes, you clench your jaw, you bounce the baby up and down, you turn your head away and pat her on the back.

What is really happening here? What is upsetting you? The many nights of being awakened, the fear of having done something wrong or the baby being ill, the broken heater that won't ever get fixed, the momentarily unhelpful partner, and the prospect of many more nights like this? This is all pretty understandably distressing.

But ask yourself again, what is *really* happening here? From the perspective of mindfulness, what is happening in the present moment without all the additional stories about it, is (1) you are tired, (2) the baby is crying, and (3) the air is cold. In this moment you are aware that you are tired, the baby is crying, and the air is cold. These facts are not necessarily good or bad—they just *are*. When viewed this way, the moment becomes more manageable.

You've got a loud train of thought going, but for a moment, if you bring your attention to your breathing, to your body, and to the present moment, the likelihood is that first you will relax your body. You might find a blanket or turn on a space heater. You might notice that you are tired. What does that feel like? Muscles weak, eyes droopy, heart a little tense. You might begin to cradle your tiredness, to sway from side to side, and allow your eyes to close.

And the crying—well, yes, it has been engineered to get your attention so it's not necessarily pleasant. But really, it's a loud sound that your baby is using to communicate some body sensation or feeling. Here you are with this loud sound. Be interested. What does it really sound like? Maybe, it's high or screechy. It sounds like a hawk's cry when it's circling overhead. Perhaps it reminds you of a blender or even of nails on a chalkboard. Meet it and relax into it. Move yourself right into the middle of it. Walk around it and find out what else is in your experience. What's in the room? Look through the window—the stars are out. There are crickets chirping. You are safe at home with your baby, despite being tired, chilly, and having some crying for a while.

When approached mindfully, even distressing experiences can be met with some degree of acceptance. And when you take an accepting stance toward the experience, your whole state of being often changes. Even when your state *remains* agitated and upset, this too can be met with mindful awareness and with fewer of the judging thoughts and anxiety-provoking stories that so often ratchet up the discomfort. By approaching the situation and your feelings about it with a willingness to have them what they are, rather than resisting them or struggling to change them, you can reduce a lot of unnecessary suffering.

how can mindful motherhood help me stay sane?

While mindful motherhood won't change a difficult-to-soothe baby, a broken heater, lack of sleep, or lots of other tough situations you'll face as a mama-to-be or new mama, what it can do is change how you relate to and respond to these situations.

In a way, mindfulness is like learning to surf. By riding the waves of experience, rather than fighting them, you get a lot less battered about. You still experience each of them, to be sure—a big wave still feels like a big wave, and a small one feels like a small one—but learning how to let go and ride the waves helps keep you from being caught up in the riptides of agitation, obsessive worrying, rage, or avoidance that can come from wrestling with those waves.

With mindful awareness, challenging situations become more manageable, not because anything changes about them or even because how you think and feel about them has changed. Instead, they become more manageable because you learn a new way of approaching your experiences—your thoughts, your feelings, your bodily sensations—allowing them to be just as they are and greeting them with friendliness, gentleness, and compassion. When you meet difficult situations with mindfulness, you get knocked off balance less often. And when you do get knocked off balance, you recover more quickly because you've learned how to remain present, aware, and connected with your baby, no matter what is happening.

Why is this? For one thing, with mindful awareness you see that almost every experience is temporary, and most experiences are very temporary. Whether it's a cramp in the lower back, labor pain, the baby crying, or a conflict with a partner, experiences (thoughts, feelings, body sensations) are always shifting and changing, like waves in the ocean. They almost never stay; and in truth, most experiences last a short amount of time—ten minutes, or an hour, tops. Rarely, there are experiences that do stay around a heck of a long time, like the grief at losing a loved one. But *most* things, the vast majority of experiences that cause us daily stress and suffering, are extremely temporary. Much of our tension, stress, and suffering come from trying to make experiences stop or trying to make them stay the same. When you get more comfortable with the fact that everything is always changing, you begin to pay more attention to riding the waves rather than struggling against them or trying to control them.

With mindful awareness, even when you are feeling sadness, fear, anger, or guilt, you have an increasing capacity to remain present, to stay connected with your baby, to be able to set nurturing limits (for both yourself and your baby), and to respond to what is actually happening rather than reacting to your story about what is happening. You are less likely to translate pure, normal, and natural emotions like sadness, fear, or anger into more chronic experiences of depression, anxiety, rage, or shame. More and more, you are able to act in alignment with your values and your goals to be the kind of mother you want to be. You are free to make choices, rather than being caught in old habit patterns.

And just as important as dealing with the challenges, mindful awareness in pregnancy and early motherhood opens the door to experiences of deep contentment, expansive joy, fierce love, and warm sensuality that can deepen the parts of pregnancy and motherhood that are enjoyable and hold the potential to be transformative. Being open to this depth of feeling can change your understanding of who you are and what you are capable of. Being able to fully attend to your present-moment experience with your baby, no matter what is happening, reveals elements of that experience that may not have been available to you before now because of all that thinking, planning, figuring out, worrying, or struggling against the parts of your experience that are not as preferable. When you learn to be fully present, meeting each experience as it is and even leaning into it, your experience of motherhood becomes more imbued with those small, transcendent moments that make all the rest of it more than worthwhile.

how can mindful motherhood help me with my baby?

A whole lot of being an effective mom rests on being able to stay in contact with your baby even when she is distressed. "Distressed" is a nice way of saying she is crying, screaming her head off, or, sometimes worse, sick in that scary way of being feverish, lethargic, and too ill to cry. Staying in contact means, in the ideal sense, that your body is warm and relaxed and you are able to return your baby's eye contact, as well as being able to maintain connection with her through your sounds, your touch, and your breathing, even when she's not happy. You are *attuned* or well-matched to your baby's mood and are able to be a kind of mirror for her—one that both recognizes her distress and conveys the message that it's okay to be feeling that way, that you can handle it, that you are not going anywhere, and that she will make it through this wave of emotion.

Staying in contact requires being able to deal with your *own* distress, whether that takes the form of tears, anger, racing thoughts, agitation, or just that generally overwhelmed, freaked-out feeling. When you practice mindful motherhood, you stretch your capacity to tolerate distress, both yours and your baby's. Mindful motherhood offers a way to deal with distress that does not ask you to try to change the content of your thinking, change what you are feeling, or change the situation. Instead, mindfulness shows you how you can relate to each situation, just as it is, with acceptance and awareness, staying present in the moment and in nurturing connection with your baby.

As you practice mindful awareness, you become more able to allow yourself or your baby to be upset and to let that state of mind be there without necessarily having to react to it immediately. You can allow distressing experiences to form, rise like a big wave, and then to eventually fade away. You can let difficult thought patterns run right on through, without necessarily needing to do anything about them. This gives you a much bigger "container" within which to hold everything that happens. And this bigger container makes all the difference. It allows you to stay present and aware and to make a choice about how to respond that is in alignment with your values and goals rather than being driven to react because it's so hard to tolerate what's happening.

This makes you more effective as a mom and your experience of motherhood more enjoyable. Over time you are more and more often able to meet what is happening as it is and to base your responses on the actual situation, rather than your stories about it, or your desire to make it stop or make it stay.

Each time you do this, you very literally transmit that capacity to your child. Your baby senses that he is safe, that you are solid, that his own overwhelming experiences are not overwhelming you. Even when you do get overwhelmed or upset, your capacity to remain present and connected with your baby lays the groundwork for him developing a strong and secure sense of self.

why now? don't I have enough on my plate?

There could not be a better time to learn mindfulness than during pregnancy and early motherhood. You are already reorganizing your lifestyle and reorienting yourself to a whole new way of being, so you might as well reorient your perspective in a way that will help you not only with parenting, but with all of the situations and experiences you encounter in life. It's something you can learn quickly, it doesn't require drugs or years of therapy, and it doesn't cost a lot of money. Becoming mindful, as a way of being, is a lifelong journey. But there are some ideas and practices that you can learn *now* that will improve your ability to deal with stress and difficult moods, to get less caught up in negative thinking patterns, and to be more available to the pleasurable moments and deep joy that motherhood can bring.

This is a time when most women have a strong motivation to become the best person they can be in a relatively short period of time. When you're struck with the enormity of the journey you have embarked upon by becoming a mom (or by having an additional child if you are already a mom), there is a really high level of motivation to try your hardest to get yourself into the best mental and emotional shape possible. After all, you will be the primary source of care for *another whole human being,* not to mention one you will love more than you ever thought possible. I've talked to many pregnant women who have, for the first time in their lives, encountered within themselves a deep and sweet drive to learn new ways of being—quickly! They don't want to pass on negative patterns to their child and want to do everything possible to transmit a healthy foundation to this new being.

Since mindfulness has a lot to do with being aware of the sensations in your body, you are in a prime state to learn it! In fact, pregnancy and early motherhood, stretch marks and hemorrhoids, nursing and sleep disturbance, weight gain and weight loss can all force you to be more *in* your body. Now is a time when you simply can't ignore all the signals your body is sending you. For those of us who live most of our lives above our necks, being required to spend more time in our bodies can be a great blessing.

This is a great time to learn mindfulness because you are already open and somewhat vulnerable. The downside of this can be feeling off balance or a little exposed, needing more help from others than usual, and being at the mercy of your body's functions and your baby's needs. The upside is that this state of being provides a sort of malleability—some of your defenses are down, and you may be feeling more sensitive than usual, so this is a great time to learn new skills! In the same way that the hormone relaxin is making your joints more flexible, your mind is also more open and flexible than when you feel like you've got everything under control.

Young infants have a way of demanding that you attend to the present moment. Even if you get distracted, a baby's needs will bring you back to the "now" again and again. And for most women, being fully engaged in the moment with a newborn baby can be extremely rewarding. Not every moment of course, and for up to about 18 percent of women who experience some level of postpartum depression (Gavin et al. 2005), not even most moments. But nearly everyone experiences a depth of love, a stretching open of the heart, a true, deep, and unshakable desire to *be with* this other little being in ways that they never had before. My mom's-group friends and I called it "baby TV." It's amazing how much time you can spend just watching a sleeping baby and smelling the warm-bread scent of her fuzzy head.

what brought me to mindfulness

My own interest in mindfulness started in my early twenties. I had a rough time of it as a teenager, encountering frequent bouts of depressive and anxious moods, ups and downs with addictive substances, and floods of negative thought patterns. While I had many potential resources to draw from for help, none seemed to completely strike home for me. Even when things smoothed out and I went to college to become a psychologist, I couldn't explain what the source of my suffering was. An awakening came for me when I started to learn about Buddhism.

The philosophy and practice of Buddhism is in large part directed toward identifying the causes of and solutions to human suffering. From this perspective, pain, imperfection, injury, impermanence, and eventually death are all natural parts of life. Suffering comes from not really accepting this fact. Instead, we are often motivated by *attachment*, grasping onto experiences and trying to make them stay, and *aversion*, or trying to get away from experiences or make them stop. With my roller-coaster ride as a young person, I experienced the painful truth in this statement. I wanted more than anything to make the good feelings of security, happiness, and even joy and ecstasy stay with me and to make the feelings of sadness, anxiety, self-hatred, and insecurity go away. My efforts to make good feelings stay and bad feelings go away paradoxically caused me more suffering than the difficult feelings themselves!

This is not a book about Buddhism, and I am not a spiritual teacher. I am a psychologist trained in how contemplative and spiritual practices and experiences contribute to psychological and emotional health and well-being. My clinical training (the foundation for how I work with clients) focused on Integral Psychology, or psychology that integrates Eastern philosophies, religious and indigenous theologies, theories of spiritual development, and subjectivity into the practice of psychology. My research training took place in a university and major medical school. There I studied addictions and the ways that difficulties dealing with emotions perceived as intolerable can lead to cravings and relapse. Along the way, my personal spirituality served as a refuge, a source of inspiration and guidance, and a stimulator of personal growth.

Buddhist thought teaches that once we experience for ourselves and see clearly the source of suffering, we can lessen and ultimately end it. It is a very practical set of guidelines for living that helps us witness the patterns that spring from a desire to have things be the way we want them to be, rather than what they actually are. By repeatedly and directly experiencing our tendencies and questioning our reactions, we allow ourselves to see more clearly and have more choices in how we behave and what we choose to focus on.

Mindfulness is one practice Buddhism offers in the service of lessening suffering and increasing health, well-being, and wholeness. But Buddhism is only one of many spiritual or philosophical traditions that emphasize contemplative or reflective practices as a pathway to greater health in yourself and your relationships. Meditation in varying forms plays a strong role in Hinduism and the yogic traditions derived from it. There is a strong historical tradition of Christian contemplative practice, and meditation is also important in Jewish and Islamic traditions. While the emphasis these traditions place on contemplative practices has been less than the emphasis on their devotional aspects such as worship and prayer, there is a recent revival of contemplative practice occurring within these traditions. *Centering prayer* is a nondenominational form of Christian meditation that is being taught in many churches around the world, and Kabbalah is a contemplative form of Judaism that has recently been revived. While these Abrahamic traditions may focus more attention to one's thoughts and experiences while in relationship with God, there are also elements of training the mind to be steady in the face of everchanging experiences—in other words, mindfulness.

It wasn't until I had my daughter that I realized how my spiritual life, particularly mindfulness practices, would help me during the transformation of pregnancy, labor, and early motherhood. I called upon those understandings and skills every day—through mood swings, back pain, stretch marks, a fifty-seven-hour labor, and relationship tensions. They not only helped me with difficult moments, but they also opened me in a profound way to the rewards of pregnancy and early mother-hood. I was able to more fully experience those exquisite moments of nursing in a rocking chair in a sun-filled room, reflections dancing on the walls, dust motes drifting in the rays of light, my daughter's toothless smile, the way she made a soft creaking sound whenever she was falling asleep (*eehhhhh, ehhhhhh, ehhhhh*). In a card a friend gave me at my baby shower she wrote, "Now your heart will stretch wide open, and you'll love beyond anything you've ever known." This was true and remains true to this day. So, I write this book as a psychologist, a researcher—and a mom.

scientific research on mindfulness

Mindfulness as a practice, and as a psychological trait or skill, has been somewhat extracted from its Buddhist roots and incorporated into interventions that have garnered a lot of interest from psychologists and cognitive scientists. Based on the observation that highly experienced meditators seemed to be able to manifest sustained ways of being that were particularly happy, peaceful, and well-adjusted, psychologists wondered if these practices might be able to enhance peace and well-being in the general population. With the knowledge that stress can cause or exacerbate all kinds of physical ailments, researchers and clinicians also wondered whether mindfulness practice might be helpful for stress-related physiological ail-ments. As a result, educational programs that train people in mindfulness skills have been developed, such as Mindfulness-Based Stress Reduction (MBSR), an eight-to-ten-week course where people learn how to practice mindfulness (Kabat-Zinn 1982). So far, the results seem very promising (Grossman et al. 2004)

Studies show that mindfulness training can improve mood, increase a sense of control, and reduce symptoms of illness in healthy individuals (Astin 1997; Rosenzweig et al. 2003; Shapiro, Schwartz, and Bonner 1998). It has been shown to decrease stress and fatigue and improve mood, sleep, and overall quality of life in cancer patients, even six months after participating in mindfulness training (Speca et al. 2000; Carlson et al. 2001; Carlson et al. 2003; Carlson and Garland 2005). A recent trial demonstrated reductions in stress symptoms and mood disturbance in caregivers of chronically ill children when the caregivers received training in MBSR (Minor et al. 2006). Mindfulness training appears to benefit people who are healthy and under normal levels of stress, as well as people who are experiencing a serious illness or high levels of stress.

MBSR has also been modified and studied as a treatment to prevent relapse in depression. In a randomized, controlled trial, the researchers reported that for patients who had had three or more previous episodes of depression, participation in a program that combined elements of mindfulness training with cognitive therapy (termed Mindfulness-Based Cognitive Therapy or MBCT) reduced the rate of relapse to approximately one-half that of patients receiving standard treatment (Teasdale et al. 2000). The benefits of MBCT to prevent relapse to depression have also been shown by Ma and Teasdale (2004), who found strikingly similar results. More recent data also suggest that mindfulness-based therapy can be effective in reducing depression in treatment-resistant patients (Kenny and Williams 2007). Finally, in a recent trial, researchers demonstrated significant reductions in depressive symptoms among fibromyalgia patients receiving training in mindfulness meditation (Sephton et al. 2007).

Teasdale and colleagues suggest that scientific evidence supports the idea that the cultivation of *metacognition*, or the capacity to be aware of your thoughts, might account for the success of mindfulness training for depression (2002). This suggests that changing one's *relationship* to negative thoughts, rather than changing their *content*, may be the key factor in preventing relapse to depression.

The positive effects of mindfulness-based interventions on negative emotions are further supported by studies carried out by Davidson and colleagues (2003). These investigators found a significant increase of activation in the left prefrontal cortex (and a corresponding decline in right prefrontal cortex activity) in a group of psychologically stressed-out high-tech workers following their participation in an eight-week MBSR program. The investigators concluded that mindfulness training was associated with a shift in brain function, from a pattern that previous data suggest reflects more negative emotions and withdrawal/avoidance to a brain-functioning pattern that reflects a more approach-oriented, positive outlook on life. This presumably positive effect on brain functioning remained in place when participants were studied six months after having received the training, suggesting that the effects are long-term. These results are particularly relevant in light of the finding that depressed mothers and their newborns show the same pattern of increased relative right-frontal activation (the withdrawal/negative emotion pattern) (Buss et al. 2003). Furthermore, immunity, as measured by antibody response to a flu shot, was improved in the mindfulness-training participants at the six-month follow-up (Davidson et al. 2003).

Based on all these results, and our own experiences as parents, my colleague John Astin and I developed the Mindful Motherhood Program. Because stress and anxiety during pregnancy are known to increase risks for detrimental outcomes (like preterm birth, low birth weight, and a less-than-optimal fetal environment), we worked on developing comprehensive mindfulness training that would address these issues directly in a way that was specific to pregnant women. Then we worked to add training components that we thought would best prepare women for what they might experience and enhance mother-infant bonding after the baby was born. Finally, we added some elements that we thought might help with childbirth.

Bringing together elements from several different mindfulness-training programs, as well as our own newly developed material, we piloted the program first in a group of ten women. After this group ended, we made some changes to the program based on participants' feedback and our experience as facilitators and researchers and tried it out on another group of women. Finally, we compared two groups of women—one that received the training in pregnancy and one that did not. The women who did not receive the training during pregnancy participated in it when their babies were between three and six months old.

Though small, this pilot study showed that it was possible to learn mindful awareness during pregnancy and early motherhood (even with baby in tow!). And we also showed that those who engaged in mindfulness training during pregnancy had reduced negative emotions and anxiety during pregnancy compared with women who did not participate in the training (Vieten and Astin 2008). There were also trends toward reduced symptoms of depression and increased positive emotion. The women in our courses were from all walks of life, and most found it an enriching experience. These are the kinds of experiences I hope you'll have reading this book.

how to use this book

This book is a practical guide for learning how cultivating mindful awareness can help you deal with the situations, thoughts, and feelings you'll encounter during your pregnancy and early motherhood. If you already practice mindfulness, this book offers ways to weave mindful awareness throughout your daily life as a new mom.

Pregnancy and early motherhood can be uniquely disruptive to your usual self-care routines, such as setting aside time for meditation or yoga. But this period of time also provides an opportunity to cultivate a practice of radical mindfulness—one that is deeply embodied, and infuses itself throughout your everyday life.

Mindfulness is moment-to-moment, nonjudgmental awareness of your present-moment experience, so that increasingly, as time goes on, you are able to approach your experience with curiosity and compassion rather than habitually reacting based on your desire for situations to be other than they are. *Mindful Motherhood* is focused on helping you be aware and stay in the present moment so that you can be connected with your baby even in times of distress, be less overwhelmed by distressing emotions and less caught up in negative thought patterns, and enjoy the simple pleasures that suffuse each day of being a mom.

This book is made up of twenty-four chapters that should take about twenty minutes each to read. You can read any one of them during a quick, feet-up rest while pregnant, one session of nursing, or an unusual moment to yourself when the baby is napping. You can read the book straight through, flip to a chapter that seems particularly appropriate to you that day, and by all means, read them over and over. Repetition is essential in developing the skill of mindfulness.

Most chapters include one or more five-to-ten-minute exercises that you can incorporate into your everyday life. You may find great times to practice when you're parked with the baby sleeping in the back of the car, when you just wake up, while nursing, during a lunch break at work, swinging your babe at the park, and even while running with the jog stroller or taking a walk.

In the first section of the book, I discuss the basics of mindful awareness and mindfulness practice in the context of pregnancy, childbirth, and early mother-hood. The next several chapters talk about the qualities of mindful awareness and how they relate to situations you might encounter as a new mom. Section 3 focuses in on specific ways to apply mindfulness practices and principles to your everyday life as a mom—and beyond.

Chapters 2 and 4 provide instruction for more formal, twenty-minute prac-tices that I encourage you to do every day to beef up those mindfulness muscles and get familiar with the territory of mindful awareness. Feel free to practice for ten minutes or even for five minutes if you don't have twenty. The key to all of this is finding realistic ways that mindfulness can be incorporated into your life as a mom. Practice when you can and as much as you can so you begin to feel the benefits more quickly.

Finally, visit my website for guided practices that you can listen to at the site, download to your digital audio player, or burn onto a CD. Use these as often as they feel helpful. Most people find when they are first practicing mindful awareness that some recorded guidance can be helpful. The website also includes more information, tips, resources, and space to chat with other moms who are practicing mindfulness (at www.mindfulmotherhood.org).

SECTION 1

Mindful
Motherhood
Basics

mindful motherhood:
you can do it

in one way, mindful motherhood is a skill that you can acquire, like learning a language or how to play the violin. Mindfulness is something you can practice and get better at, and the more you practice (especially in times that are not so difficult), the more you will be able navigate the difficult moments. But mindful motherhood is more than just a practice, or a skill you can learn. It's also a *way of being*.

Being mindful is an approach to life. It is a way of viewing the world that recognizes that *things are exactly as they are*, all the time, and no amount of thinking, internal struggling, resistance, wishing it weren't that way, or hoping it will always be that way will change the fact that things are the way they are in each moment. This recognition brings an increased willingness to meet each experience fully, as a mom and in the rest of your life, with open eyes and an open heart.

The good news about mindfulness as a way of being, in contrast to seeing it as a practice you have to learn, is that *there is already a part of you that is completely and perfectly mindful* without needing to be taught or trained in any way. Your pure awareness, at its most basic level, *is mindful*. Mindfulness is the completely unadorned way that you notice what is present.

And this, as a way of being, is something you already know how to do without having to be taught. Being mindful will come naturally to you because your most basic, fundamental awareness, the part of you that is awake right now and knows it, is already inherently mindful. Mindful awareness is something you are fully capable of because your own basic awareness meets each experience as it is, without evaluation or judgment, with a sense of openness, and is curious about what arises. But experiencing things without the habitual layer of comment or judgment can feel unfamiliar.

When viewed in this way, mindful awareness does not need to be "learned" in the traditional sense. It already exists, so you don't have to create it. But moving it in a particular way, exercising it on a daily basis, will strengthen it. From this perspective, the main function of mindful awareness practice is to spend more time in mindful awareness.

The best way to become more familiar with a territory is to spend a bunch of time there. I could tell you all about the Peruvian Amazon, or the Serengeti, or Cairo. But only by spending time there would you get to know the lay of the land, learn how to find your way around, learn to speak some of the language, to navigate through sticky spots, and to get comfortable with the cultural customs. Mindful awareness practice allows you to explore a territory of your being that may be unfamiliar, that you may not have spent a lot of time in, and by spending time there, it can become a second home for you.

you are already mindful

Try this experiment. For the next few breaths, simply be aware at the barest level of yourself reading this book. Just, "Here I am, reading this book." Notice your surroundings as an objective reporter would—"There is a tree; here is a table; I'm sitting on a chair; the air is cool." Just notice whatever you naturally notice, and note it as though you were going to report it to someone else, without judgment or evaluation. Just the facts. That is mindfulness.

Now, if you had been given a few more breaths, the likelihood is you would have begun to very naturally comment on what you noticed. "It's too cold. I've always hated this plant. I don't really get this book. I like lying here in bed." There is a layer of evaluation that you very habitually add to each experience. And for the most part, it is this second layer of evaluation that causes us trouble—not the experience itself.

This is not to say that some experiences are not painful, even nearly intolerable. The death of a loved one, seeing your child in pain, intense conflict with a partner, true fear for your safety—all of these bring up raw emotions that can be very distressing. And mindfulness, for all its usefulness, does not remove that kind of pain.

But these kinds of extreme events are rare. For the most part, when whatever you are experiencing is seen without evaluating it, comparing it to the past, projecting into the future, determining what it means, or wishing it were different— most of our experiences are manageable. Even difficult experiences can at times be strangely enjoyable when encountered with curiosity and compassion.

Mindful motherhood is a way of being. It's a way of relating to all of your experiences and those of your baby with an attitude of letting them be just as they are. But this way of being is unfamiliar for most of us. It may be different from the way we were taught to be, and in some ways it conflicts with the way we are hardwired. Like learning any new habit or skill, *it takes practice*. The good news is that mindful awareness can be integrated into your everyday life in ways that are realistic during pregnancy and early motherhood.

When you're learning anything new, like how to play an instrument or how to speak a new language, you need a lot of practice. To get really good at it can take years. At the same time, if you practice any one of these skills each day, even just twenty minutes per day, you'll get a surprisingly long way with it.

It's kind of like strengthening a bicep. If you do curls for just twenty minutes per day, each day for eight weeks, you'll have a pretty good bicep built up. If you stop practicing, your bicep muscle will gradually become weaker. But then, if you begin to practice again, your "muscle memory" will make it even easier to build up when you return to practicing.

Research is beginning to show that you can train your brain in the same way (Begley 2007). Neuronal pathways that are used more often become stronger, and in a way, become lubricated with repeated use—they fire more easily. Pathways that are not used become weakened over time and become less likely to fire. Repeated mindful awareness practice is like laying down a mindfulness groove that you can begin to slip into more easily. And as a bonus, as your mindful awareness groove gets easier to access, those old habit patterns are accessed less often (worry, rumination, distraction, avoidance, self-abuse, and so on), and their pathways don't get triggered quite as easily as they used to.

As you may have noticed, it's hard for the thinking mind to wrap itself around mindfulness. This is partly because mindfulness doesn't happen in the thinking mind! So learning about it by reading alone is limited. No words can substitute for your own subjective, embodied experience of mindful awareness.

If you'd never eaten an orange, I could tell you about one all day long—the way it smells so fresh, the smooth, cool firmness of the peel, the way it squirts juice into your mouth when you bite into it. But nothing would be able to describe it better than simply giving you an orange to eat. Nothing I can tell you in this book will take the place of what you can discover for yourself through repeated mindful awareness practice and open-minded self-inquiry.

basic mindful awareness practice

There are three primary practices that this book will focus on. Try to practice one of them a little bit every day while you're reading this book. If you find them helpful, I hope you'll continue. They are:

- Mindful-awareness practice while sitting quietly, or meditation (see chapters 2 and 3)

- Mindful movement in the form of yoga (see chapter 4)

- Mindful awareness in everyday life (exercises throughout the book)

Each of the practices is helpful in its own way, and I encourage you to engage in all three. If you like, you can alternate between sitting quietly and mindful movement from day to day and try a couple of the everyday life practices each day. Or, on busy days, do a little practice whenever you can fit it in. The point is to visit the territory of mindful awareness often, and flex that mindful-awareness muscle a little bit every day.

Carving Out Time for Practice

Here's the point in the book where, if I were reading, I'd start to get a pretty familiar feeling with one of two accompanying trains of thought:

Thought 1: "Wow, this is great! I am definitely going to practice this every single day, no question about it. I'll wake up earlier, yeah! I've always wanted to be one of those people who wakes up at 6 a.m. and has a cup of tea, meditates, does a little yoga. Hey, actually, while I'm at it, I'll sign up for that Pilates class at 7 a.m. down the street..."

Thought 2: "Crap, I knew there was a catch to all this. Daily practice? Is this woman out of her mind? Does she know what real life is like? I can't get my moisturizer on reliably every day, much less find twenty minutes to practice something that I don't even understand! Forget it. I'll give this book to my sister when she gets pregnant..."

If you've got either one of these thoughts or some variation going, I invite you to *hold your horses*. I am not asking you to make a New Year's resolution around this; after all, they almost never work (as you may have noticed). Mindful motherhood is not a project. It's not a goal or a new way to become someone different from who you already are. Mindful motherhood is a set of qualities that you can choose to become more and more familiar with over time. It's a way of being that you can tune into more and more often as time goes on.

The key to integrating mindful awareness practice into your everyday life is to set a reasonable intention for daily practice and, as quickly as possible, to make it something as mundane and regular as brushing your teeth. There are many ways to make it easier to find the time to practice. Here are a few:

- After you drop off your baby at day care (and your other kids at school, if applicable), spend ten to twenty minutes practicing in the car.

- Practice while you are nursing or feeding the baby.

- Before you go to sleep, or right when you wake up, practice.

- Get one of those big physical-therapy balls, and when your baby is fussing, hold her and bounce up and down while you practice.

- When you go to the toilet, take five extra minutes and practice (if you are pregnant, this will mean you'll get all kinds of practice in!).

- Practice at the gym on the StairMaster, matching your breathing to your footsteps.

- Practice while walking with the baby in a stroller or in a front-carrier. Each time your foot touches the ground, give the action the same attention as your breathing.

- Practice with eyes open while waiting for a bus or in the waiting room at the doctor's office.

- If you are partnered, ask your partner to take turns putting the baby to bed or getting up with the baby in the morning, and practice during that time.

- If you are a single mom, ask another mom or one of those great-with-kids-but-childless or mom-whose-kids-are-grown friends to hang with the baby for a half hour while you practice in their bedroom or on their patio.

- When you eat lunch, take ten minutes before or after eating to practice.

- If you are pumping breast milk, practice (that lovely cow-milking-machine sound can actually become a nice repetitive focus of attention along with the breath).

- Practice when you are in the shower.

- When you lie down for a nap, practice.

- When the baby is napping, go to a quiet corner and practice. Or stay next to the baby with one hand on his back and practice.

- When you are at the playground, park the baby on a blanket under a tree and practice.

The trick here is to not make practicing a big deal. Find the pockets of time already in your life that are available and will work for you. Don't see mindful awareness as a serious endeavor that is separate from the rest of your life. Don't make it precious—in the "big-and-important" sense of the word. That's one way the mind resists doing something it's not familiar with.

You can use the practices in this book in many ways. You can rotate them, using one each day, or mix and match. You can practice them for twenty minutes or up to an hour, or practice them for brief periods throughout your day. Practice whenever you get the chance. Take twenty minutes, ten, five, or even two minutes. Let mindful awareness begin to creep into your everyday life. You can try setting your computer calendar or watch to alert you every hour or two throughout the day, reminding yourself to do a few minutes of mindful awareness practice. Or you can make any difficult moment a cue to stop and practice five or ten minutes of mindful awareness.

At the same time, I recommend that you *do* make each period of mindful awareness practice precious—in the sacred, silent, self-loving sense of the word. Recognize that each time you practice mindful awareness, whether sitting quietly, doing yoga, or in your daily life, you are committing to a way of being that increases your capacity to remain present and connected with your baby, curious and compassionate, solid and grounded in the face of whatever comes up.

You are training yourself to be present for your baby—for her vaccinations, fevers, sore throats, tummy aches, and itchy rashes, and for learning to navigate that gaping divide between wakefulness and sleep. You are also training yourself to be present for yourself, in the face of criticism from your mother-in-law, conflicts with friends or partners, when the car breaks down, those scary moments where you are not sure what's going on with your baby, or the pain of labor. You are beefing up your ability to be your best self, the best mom you can be.

2

mindful awareness of breathing

the first practice, being aware of your breathing for a period of time each day, is one of the best ways to cultivate mindfulness, both as a skill and as a way of being.

For some, meditation can seem hopelessly unfamiliar. You may think of it as mysterious or exotic. You may worry that meditating is contrary to your religious tradition. Or maybe you've always considered practicing meditation as just for those crunchy-granola types in California. I invite you to let go of all of those ideas.

On the other hand, if you are familiar with meditation and have strong beliefs about it—what it is and what it's not, how and where and when it should be done, who should teach it, or what gear you need to do it—I invite you to let go of those ideas as well, at least while you're reading this book.

For purposes of this book, meditation is:

> **Sitting quietly**
> **while paying attention to your experience,**
> **allowing it to be just as it is.**

It sounds simple, and it is. But for most of us, it's not easy. At first it can be uncomfortable. Over time, it gets easier (and then sometimes harder and then easier again), and it can become a comfortable and familiar refuge.

Actually, just like being a mom (and just like life in general), sitting quietly and being aware of your experience can be pleasant, unpleasant, or neutral. It can feel easy, hard, or just sort of okay. Sometimes motherhood is extremely pleasant and rewarding, sometimes it is challenging and difficult, and sometimes it's just okay. The idea here is to develop the capacity to be aware, present in the moment, and connected with your baby, no matter what is going on. You are going to start by practicing being aware and present while breathing, no matter what happens in your experience.

In the beginning, I highly recommend that you go to the Mindful Motherhood website (www.mindfulmotherhood.org) to access recorded audio guidance for each of these practices. You can practice near your computer, burn the guided meditations to a compact disc, or download them to your iPod or MP3 player (ask your nearest teenager for help, or use the instructions on the website). If you don't have access to any of these, you can order one of our compact discs by mail, which include several guided mindful motherhood practices.

The reason I recommend audio guidance when you're getting started is that it works a little bit like training wheels. When you are learning to ride a bike, it's natural to swerve all over the place, fall down, get confused about how to brake or shift gears, and so on. The same is true for learning mindful awareness. The audio guidance helps to gently keep you on course.

mindful awareness of breathing

Breathing is a great thing to place your attention on because (1) it's always happening, (2) it's always happening in the present moment, (3) it's happening in your body, and (4) it happens without your help. Paying attention to your breathing is a way to bring your attention to the present moment, to your embodied experience (rather than, or at least in addition to, the experience in your thinking mind), and to bring your attention to a process that you don't need to do anything about. You can use your breathing as a target of attention to help you learn how to be present in the moment and in your body.

Here is some guidance that is short enough for you to remember on your own. You don't need any gear, any special cushion or place, any particular bell or music—just a place to sit where you are safe. Your environment doesn't even need to be particularly quiet. It's great to learn to practice mindful awareness with noise, because when you have children, quiet, uninterrupted time can be hard to come by! It's sort of like the wisdom of not demanding complete silence for your baby's naptime or bedtime—you want to build her capacity to fall asleep even when the vacuum cleaner is running! You'll also want to build your capacity for mindful awareness even when circumstances aren't ideal.

Now try this simple breathing meditation:

Sit with your ribcage lifted up off of your belly. If you want to, sit with your back against a wall, in a straight-backed chair with your feet on the floor, or on the floor with the bottom of your spine resting on a firm pillow or folded-up blankets. Square your shoulders, dropping them slightly, and tuck your chin in a bit. Close your eyes, or if you prefer, soften your focus on a point about three to four feet in front of you.

Bring your awareness to breathing. Let your attention rest gently on your breath as it goes in and out. Let your awareness rest on your breathing just lightly, like a butterfly alighting on a flower. This is not a piercing concentration on the breath. Rather, just let your awareness saturate the process of breathing, like water sinking into a sponge.

At some point you may find that your attention drifts to some other aspect of experience, such as thinking, sounds, or a body sensation other than breathing. This is fine. Just notice that your attention has wandered and start being aware of breathing again. No need to wrestle your attention back—just gently come back to breathing.

Let all of your experiences be just as they are. Let the breath be as it is. Let your train of thought chug along. Let your body sensations be there, just as they are, without evaluating them or needing to do anything about them. For this brief period, there is nowhere to go and nothing to do. Let any sounds, sights (even when your eyes are closed), scents, or feelings be there, exactly as they are. Meet them with an open mind and an open heart. Let any emotions be there—let them come in and fade away, or come in and take up residence. Then gently return your attention to your breathing.

That's it for now. If it helps, set a timer and start by doing this breathing meditation for five minutes. Then try ten. Then try twenty. The guided meditations on our website and CDs are about twenty to twenty-five minutes long. You can practice for as long as you like. Some people find it very useful to practice for a period of time in the morning and again in the evening. The more often you can set aside blocks of time to practice, the more familiar you will become with mindful awareness and the easier it will be to access mindful awareness in your everyday life as a mom.

If you tend toward a lack of discipline or have difficulty doing things that are good for you despite your best intentions, be gentle but firm with yourself. Try to find at least one way you can engage in this practice for even a few minutes each day. Link it to something you already do, like eating or brushing your teeth, so it just becomes another ordinary activity.

On the other hand, if you tend toward overachieving and perfectionism, toward overcontrol or setting unrealistic goals for yourself, I suggest that you do no more than thirty minutes per day to begin with, and be twice as gentle as I've described. At the end of this book, there are resources you can access for more formal and intensive mindfulness training. These practices take place over longer periods of time and include guidance from very experienced teachers. This kind of training can be extremely valuable, but it's not what we're working on in this book. Letting go and being gentle and friendly with yourself is at least as valuable as determination and perseverance in mindful motherhood.

3

the ever-changing river
of experience

one of the great things about sitting quietly while paying attention to your experience, allowing it to be just as it is, is that you can see how much your changing states actually spring from your own mind rather than from changing external circumstances. When you're just sitting there, what's happening around you isn't changing very much. But, if you are like me, you'll find your experience goes all over the place.

For example, I recall one time I was practicing mindful awareness while nursing my four-week-old baby. It took about twenty minutes to nurse, and I was sitting in a rocking chair watching the dust motes float around in a beam of sunlight coming in through the window. My daughter latched on, I got that little shot of oxytocin (the feel-good mom hormone), and I felt absolutely at peace, very content, and happy. As I sat there noticing my breathing, my attention began to wander away into thinking.

I thought about a friend I had invited over a couple of weeks prior who couldn't make it. We had rescheduled for another day, but I had forgotten to write down the new date. Having new-mama mind, I completely forgot about our plan and was out with the baby when my friend came by, having driven across town to come see us. She called and left a message, understandably a bit frustrated.

I felt guilty and, at the same time, a little annoyed myself. Unfortunately, it was a friend who I hadn't kept in close touch with, and I already felt a bit tense around her. As I thought about it, a flush of shame came over me for not being a good friend and wasting her time. There was also anger. After all, she didn't have kids, so she didn't know what it was like the first several weeks after birth. She was being intolerant, unforgiving! My oxytocin was replaced by cortisol (the stressed-out hormone), and I felt agitated, a bit miserable, and literally lost in thought—not aware or present for any of it.

My daughter popped off, and I was brought back to awareness. I was amazed to see how in one twenty-minute session, I'd gone from bliss to misery with nothing at all changing except my thoughts.

getting rid of static cling

When you practice mindful awareness, you can see pretty clearly how your experiences are temporary—how they are always changing. You can see how your train of thought just keeps chugging along, apparently all on its own, with no real stimulation from the outside. You can see how trains of thought that are fed or locked into, whether with grasping (wanting them to stay) or resistance (wanting to make them stop), pick up speed and power. It also becomes clear that thought trains that are not fed or engaged seem to roll right on through.

Sometimes emotions, thoughts, and sensations seem to stick like Velcro. They can be pretty intense, can feel distressing, and can last for a while. They demand our attention, and like the cry of a newborn child, it can feel like they demand it until we do something about them. If there's nothing we can do, they just hang out like unwelcome guests, popping up to grab our attention again as soon as we've got a free minute.

Mindful awareness practice can help you to cultivate a way of relating to your train of thought so that you don't accidentally end up in Chicago because you couldn't resist jumping onto a particularly compelling railcar on the train. Or, if you do hop on the train without meaning to, you can notice you are on it and know where you are.

After all, sometimes it seems almost warm and cozy to get all involved in that familiar place of worrying about a problem. But with mindfulness practice, your consciousness becomes a little less full of static, where anything with a little charge can cling and not let go. As you practice watching the contents of the stream of experience go by, you are learning not to bite on the fishhook and get caught by a thought, however tempting it might be.

sitting on the riverbank

Sitting quietly while developing the capacity to remain present and aware of your experiences, allowing them to be just as they are, is a foundational mindful motherhood practice. It allows you to train your attention and get more familiar with that territory of mindful, present, nonevaluative awareness with minimal distractions from the outside. It provides opportunities to observe and inquire into the nature of the thinking mind and to re-establish the center of your being in the part of you that is *aware* of that thinking mind and all the other sensations you might have.

The focus of this mindful awareness practice is to simply observe various aspects of your experience as they are happening, and nothing else. The goal is not to relax, to calm down, to find a place of inner peace and contentment—though these things could happen. But this practice can also feel uncomfortable, unfamiliar, or even boring. Whatever happens in your experience, whether pleasant or unpleasant, just notice it. This is the practice.

> **Noticing what is happening in the present moment is the foundation of mindfulness.**

Observing, noticing, and exploring are natural abilities we had as little children. Have you ever seen a toddler catch sight of a beetle trundling by? It can capture the little one's attention for several minutes as he takes in everything about that beetle, watching closely. Then he can just as easily hop up and continue to toddle along the road. This practice is a little like that. Just watch closely with interest.

A good way to give your observing-and-noticing (rather than thinking-and-doing) muscle a workout is to practice observing the thoughts, feelings, and sensations in your body during times that are relatively neutral, when you aren't upset or wildly happy. Try it when there isn't a lot going on. Practicing in neutral times makes you more prepared to notice and observe your experience when you encounter difficult moments or when big feelings come up.

You might wonder how this could help you. Well, the capacity for observing, noticing, or being aware of what is happening in your present-moment experience is the beginning of being able to remain present and connected to your baby even in times of difficulty or distress. You will be exercising your capacity to meet each experience with a sense of openness, curiosity, and compassion, to let it be as it is without struggling against it, trying to make it stay, or trying to make it go away. And however simple observing experiences might seem, it actually can take quite a bit of practice.

Try this meditation now:

Take a moment to sit up and lift your ribcage off of your abdomen. This is easier said than done when pregnant, I know. But propping a pillow behind your lower back or even under your arms can help. Now breathe. Notice your breathing as it goes in and out. Just notice it, without changing it. If the breathing begins to change on its own, notice that.

Now notice what you are hearing. Hear it just as it is for the moment, not even needing to name it. If you automatically name it, that's fine. But try to simply notice it and then see if you hear anything else. Make your hearing keen—hear the soft, subtle sounds as well as the loud ones. The humming of the refrigerator. A bird singing. Cars going by. The tick-tock of a clock. Your own breathing.

Notice next what you see. If your eyes are closed, you can note what's happening there behind your eyelids. Or, if you open your eyes, just soften your focus and notice what you see. If naming each thing you see with one word is useful, do that. Chair. Tree. My knees. My baby. Just take note of what is in your field of vision.

Next, notice anything you taste. You may not have eaten anything recently, but you might taste a little bit of something. Metallic. Garlicky. Kind of neutral. Notice any tastes that are present in this moment.

Now notice anything you smell. Breathe in deeply through your nose and let any scents, however pungent or subtle, be noticed. For now, don't attend to whether or not you like them or dislike them. Just recognize the process of smelling.

Now, what do you feel? Is your body pressing against the bed, floor, or chair? Is there warmth or coolness? Tension in any part of the body? The baby within, or the baby on your lap or next to you? Air against your skin? Just take note of any tactile or physical sensations.

Next, notice your thoughts. You may be thinking any number of things. Just notice them as they go by.

Now notice your feelings. Are there any emotions? Contentment? Boredom? Sadness? Anger? Guilt? Just notice, with lightness, each feeling you are having right now, in the present moment.

Now return to your breathing. Notice your breath going in and out for a few more breaths.

Let each of your experiences pass through, like leaves floating down a stream. You can decide to pick up a leaf and examine it, but then put it back into the stream. Or just let them all float on by.

Notice anything that may have changed about your breathing, other sensations, your thoughts, your feelings, or your general state of being after engaging in this practice. Has anything shifted?

The whole point of this practice is to notice what is happening in your experience *right now*. As you get used to this kind of meditation, you'll find that it is very powerful for bringing you into mindful awareness—in the present moment, in your body, and in connection with your baby.

mindful motherhood
yoga series

Jnana Gowan coauthored this chapter. She is a certified yoga instructor who specializes in working with prenatal and postpartum moms, and she developed the Mindful Motherhood Yoga Series.

Jnana brings a wealth of personal and professional experience to this work. As a mom, she has integrated a mindfulness practice into her daily life with the help of her son, Riley. You can learn more about Jnana's work with individuals, groups, and in the corporate setting in the resources section at the end of this book. The Mindful Motherhood Yoga Series in this chapter was illustrated by another great mom, Joanne Le Cocq, a professional designer and artist.

awareness while moving

Bringing attention to the sitting body is one thing (and most people are surprised by how much is going on just when sitting quietly), but bringing attention to the present moment, the breath, and the body *while moving* is a whole other ball of wax. As a mom, you will be moving a lot. The Mindful Motherhood Yoga Series is designed to help you practice being present, aware, and connected with your baby, not only while you are sitting quietly, but also while you are moving around.

If there is a teacher in your area who is familiar with pre- or postnatal yoga, you may want to join her class if that is an option for you. Pre- and postnatal yoga classes are increasingly offered in gyms, community centers, yoga studios, and mind-body health clinics for those who would like to engage in more intensive practice. For many women, a prenatal or mom-baby yoga class is their first experience of yoga.

When they're pregnant, some women feel as though nothing much has changed—that they are just gaining weight. Others can barely lift their heads off a pillow, have lots of aches and pains, or cannot turn the nausea off. Being in a room with other women having similar experiences can be very empowering. It's a great way to meet other new moms, which is another big key to staying balanced in pregnancy and early motherhood.

We chose yoga for the Mindful Motherhood Training because it is a mindful movement practice that has evolved over millennia, and a curriculum has been developed for pre- and postnatal women that research shows is safe and beneficial for the childbearing years. Mindful yoga is particularly powerful for learning to work with your breath, get into your body, and cultivate present-moment awareness. But if you prefer, you can engage in other forms of mindful movement such as tai chi or qigong, or less formal practices like walking, dancing, biking, or simply stretching. For example, to practice mindful awareness while walking, rather than while sitting quietly, you can modify the awareness-of-breathing practice in chapter 2 by replacing the word "breathing" with "walking" and replacing "each breath" with "each step." You can also download walking meditation audio guidance at the website. If you have any concerns about your physical ability to do any of the practices, check with your physician before beginning.

The kind of yoga most Westerners are familiar with is *hatha* yoga, or the physical aspect of yoga such as postures and breath work (or *pranayama*). The postures themselves are known as *asanas*, so the practice itself may be referred to as an "asana practice." In Sanskrit, the word *yoga* means to "yoke" or unite. When embarking upon the hatha yoga path, the practitioner works to unite the mind, the body, and the spirit. This is exactly what pregnancy and early motherhood calls for—finding a balance between your body, your mind, and your spirit or deeper self. This is the practice that we will explore in this chapter.

The Sanskrit word for "breathing" is *prana*. But more than breathing, prana refers to your life force, your sense of aliveness—the primordial energy that underlies the mental, physical, and spiritual health and strength of all things. When you practice yoga, you use your breath as a bridge between your body and your mind. Your mind is given the task of paying attention to your breathing and connecting you more deeply to your true self, that place of awareness that is beyond your thoughts, feelings, or bodily sensations. Awareness of breathing acts as an anchor, bringing you into the current moment.

Doing even a small amount of yoga prior to sitting meditation can be extremely helpful. In the Mindful Motherhood Training Program, we begin each class with twenty minutes of yoga. It helps to rein the busy thinking mind into the present moment, centers us into our bodies, and allows us to arrive fully in a quieter, more focused place.

As you practice mindful yoga, you will move your body into specific poses and hold them for a period of time. For example, in warrior pose you'll bring mindful awareness to your breath and your body while you stand with legs spread and arms out wide. In class, this pose is held up to one minute (about the length of a typical labor contraction), and it can be quite challenging. Many women say that while holding this rigorous pose, they find new ways to ground and center themselves. Through breath work, determination, and letting go, these women learn to lean into the pose rather than tensing up against it. Practicing creates an "I can do it!" attitude (which is very beneficial for a woman who is moving toward birthing a baby).

Many situations in motherhood are like warrior pose. For example, those moments when you have a baby on one hip and are attempting to untangle your toddler from her carseat while helplessly watching as an open bottle of freshly pumped breastmilk spills onto the carpet of your car. Or sitting in traffic at a dead stop, late to pick up the baby from child care, while you watch your cell phone drain itself of its last little bit of battery power. These stressful situations can be approached with the same kind of "lean-into-it" warrior stance that mindful yoga cultivates. And labor—well, labor may be the biggest warrior pose you'll ever encounter in your life, and being able to breathe and be present through it is incredibly helpful.

As my midwife said to me, "You can't think a baby out of your body." Birthing books and classes may be helpful in an educational way, or even just to get you thinking about labor. But when labor begins, it comes down to you, the baby, and your breath.

the mindful motherhood yoga series

The Mindful Motherhood Yoga Series does not require taking a lot of time away from your regular routine. It can be done when you wake up, prior to falling asleep, during your lunch hour, before or after a workout or walk, while hanging out with your baby—any time. It is a quick and easy way to engage in mindful movement and is something that will hopefully feed your soul.

As with any exercise or movement program, a few words should be said regarding your safety. There's a baby in there, or there was very recently! While you are pregnant, one thing that is physically different is that your placenta is causing the hormone *relaxin* to course through your body. Relaxin softens the connective tissue and ligaments in your body, making yoga a perfect accompaniment to this hormonal change. This suppleness of the body is at its peak in pregnancy, and this can allow you to overstretch.

This is not a "no pain, no gain" practice. This is a time to slow down and connect with your breath, your body, and the baby. As soon as you feel any tension nearing pain, reduce the stretch slightly and hold the pose there. Pay attention to your breathing. If your breath is straining in a pose, slow down. If you are grunting as you move, ease up. Also, if you feel uncomfortable doing a pose or it feels like it is too much, discontinue the pose and ask your health practitioner for his or her opinion. You can also ask for the guidance of a professional yoga instructor who can observe you in person. Also, discontinuing a particular pose for a bit and then trying it later in the pregnancy may work. The body is changing so rapidly that the pose may be difficult at a particular time and okay a little farther down the road.

Practicing mindful movement makes you into an explorer. With your ever-changing pregnant and postpartum body, there is a vast arena available for exploration. Every day is different; your belly expanding or contracting, "mystery" pains, shifting or gaining weight—all of these changes are an invitation to connect with your new self and your baby.

You may encounter strong emotions when you begin working with the breath and mindfully moving. You may find places of tension in your body that you have been holding, often without realizing it. When this happens, you may experience feelings of sadness, anger, or just a general discomfort that is hard to discern. Without trying to change your experience (as may be your first impulse), see if you can stay with these feelings and emotions. Breathe into them and observe how they all eventually change.

You don't *need* any gear to do this mindful yoga series, but you might find it helpful to get a yoga mat (highly recommended because it will help keep you from slipping). Other items to consider are: three or four thick, sturdy books or yoga blocks (which can be found in a yoga studio, online, or in one of the big superstores), two firm blankets or large towels, a chair, and a stool. You may not need all of these items, depending on how you move through the session. But especially during pregnancy, you may find that the bigger you get, the more helpful these props will be.

This session is designed to take about twenty to thirty minutes. We recommend that you do the series in its entirety. You can download a "cheat sheet" with all of the poses on one page at our website. But because mindful motherhood is about weaving these practices into your everyday life as a mom, on the days that you just do not have the time (or energy) to complete the entire practice, you may break the series into one of two sections: the seated poses or the standing poses. And you can always practice a few of your favorite poses when you get a few minutes, particularly if you are feeling stuck, lethargic, achy, or bloated.

You can do this series with your baby. Though it is ideal to carve out time for yourself, don't wait for alone time to practice yoga, because that may be a rarity. Go ahead and include your baby in your practice. Besides, babies love to watch their moms get into crazy positions! Do some of the poses over your baby lying on the mat (carefully) or while he is lying on his back next to you for the sitting poses. It can be another sweet way to connect mindfully with your little one.

Last, because the pose names tend to vary when using a Western description, we use the Sanskrit name for each pose first and a popular Western term second.

Note: if you are anything like me, this is the point where I would flip through the next several pages, thinking "That looks great!" and "I'll give it a try sometime." I encourage you to try it now.

Part One: Sitting Poses

Sukhasana: Easy Pose

Sit on one or two firm blankets or a very firm pillow. Sit on your "sits" bones (the bones in your behind) with crossed legs. With sits bones connected to the ground, lift from each side of your waist up to your armpits to lengthen the spine. Breathe. Settle in, taking three to five cycles of breathing.

Part One

Inhale and raise your arms up with palms up. Next, turn your palms to face out. Exhale and lower arms down with palms down. Palms up, inhale, arms up. Then palms down, exhale, arms down. Repeat three to five times. You may want to practice by counting from one to six as you inhale and exhale to slow your breath down.

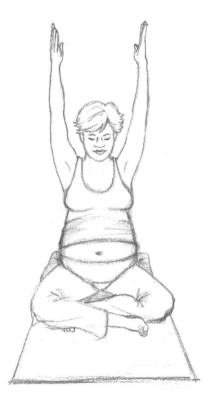

Part Two

Inhale and raise your arms up, bringing palms together. Now interlace your fingers, and on your exhale, turn your palms toward the ceiling. Stay for one or two full breaths, then release your arms down.

Part Three (not shown)

Inhale, bringing your arms behind your back and interlacing your fingers, palms facing one another. When you exhale, straighten your arms back, hands clasped together, lift your chest up, and stay there for one or two breaths.

Repeat **part two** with arms overhead, switching the interlace of fingers so that the opposite thumb is in front. Then, repeat **part three** with opposite interlace.

Upavista Konasana: Straddled Open-Legs Pose

Open your legs wide, into a straddle. Inhale, stretching your arms over your head, keeping them shoulder-width apart with palms facing one another. Reach up through your pinky and ring finger. Keep the legs fully engaged by flexing your toes toward your face and keeping your knees pointed toward the ceiling.

Now exhale, bringing your right hand to the floor as the left arm reaches up and stays in line with your torso. The hand on the floor will support you in the next move. Now side-stretch to the right with your left arm. Inhale, come up to center, bringing both arms over your head once again. Exhale and repeat on the opposite side.

Baddha Konasana: Butterfly/Tailor Sitting Pose

From the previous pose, with your legs straddled, bring your legs together. Reach your hands inside each knee and pull your knees toward you, bringing the soles of your feet together at the heels, six to twelve inches from the groin.

Part One

Hold onto your ankles and begin rotating your torso around in circles. Synchronize your breath as you rotate around, inhaling as you rotate back and exhaling as you rotate forward. When doing this pose, *do not push your knees to the floor.* Continue to press the balls of your feet and inner heels into one another as you rotate in circles. If you are pregnant, you may feel like you are squishing the baby, so do only what is comfortable for the two of you. Do this for five cycles of breathing, then repeat in the opposite direction. When complete, come into a neutral, seated position.

Part Two

Hold onto your ankles as you inhale and tip your pelvis forward. Draw your shoulder blades down your back toward the floor, arching your spine into a backbend. Bring your gaze upward toward the ceiling, lifting your chin gently.

Exhale, and continuing to hold your ankles, roll back onto your sacrum (the base of your spine), rounding your back and straightening your arms, breathing into a deep stretch in the upper back. Synchronize your breath as you roll forward and back for five to ten cycles of breathing. Inhale, lifting your chest as you go into the slight backbend. Now exhale and roll back, rounding your back and straightening your arms.

Adho Mukha Svanasana: Downward-Facing Dog

Come onto your hands and knees, with your fingers spread. Turn your hands out slightly, at about a 45-degree angle. Place your knees and feet about hips-width apart, maybe slightly wider if you are pregnant. Finding the right stance can take some practice. If your feet are too close, you may feel tension in your spine, and if they are too far apart you may end up overworking. Take a breath in and, as you exhale, turn your toes so that they are flat on the ground and straighten the legs, keeping all ten toes facing forward. Reach your hands into the floor as you lengthen your tailbone away from your skull. Press all four points of your palms into the floor, keeping your elbows in. Release your head and let it hang down between your arms. Stay in this pose for three to five breaths only. If you feel dizzy or lightheaded, come down and rest in Child's Pose (to follow). *Do not continue to do this pose if you are feeling dizzy or lightheaded.*

Note: If you are just beginning this practice, if you are quite pregnant, or both, then this pose may feel like too much for you. If so, skip it and go to the next pose. With your changing body comes the invitation to mindfully check in with where you are each day.

Adho Mukha Virasana: Child's Pose

Moving from Downward Dog, come back down to all fours, on your hands and knees. Bring your big toes together, keeping your knees apart, and then sit your hips down onto your heels (keeping legs wide enough for your belly to come in between if you are pregnant). As you exhale, release into a forward bend. You may want to walk your hands forward, resting your belly between your legs. Continue to draw the shoulder blades down your back, reaching your arms overhead with your palms on the floor. Even as you rest on your heels, continue to reach your tailbone back toward your heels. If you are able, rest your forehead on the floor. Women with bigger bellies may prop themselves up on their elbows (or a pillow) and let the head release down.

Note: You may go from Downward-Facing Dog to Child's Pose three to five times.

Part Two: Standing Poses

Uttanasana: Standing Forward Bend

From Child's Pose, roll your toes under with your stance wider than hips'-width apart. Keeping your hands on the floor (or on books/blocks or a chair) for support, straighten your legs, lifting your hips up and letting your head down. Hanging from the hip crease, let the weight of your head draw you toward the floor. Keep your hips and heels in line as you release the head toward the floor. Engage the flesh above the knees, tightening and drawing the thigh muscles up. The more you work your legs, the more your spine will release. Imagine that you are hanging from your hips as much as possible, allowing the spine to release. Let the back of your knees open, and breath deeply, as though you were inhaling all the way into the backs of your thighs.

To come out of this pose: Bend your knees slightly, then bring your hands onto your thighs for additional support as you roll up to Tadasana (Mountain Pose), described next.

Tadasana: Mountain Pose

Maintaining a pre-pregnant posture throughout pregnancy and postpartum is very helpful as you gain weight and your body boundaries expand out. As part of

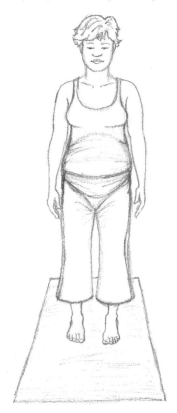

your daily mindfulness practice, do this pose while waiting in line at the grocery store or the bank, or while waiting for a bus or taxi.

Stand with your feet hips'-width apart, with the outsides of your feet almost parallel. Bring your heels out slightly. Press your feet evenly into the floor and spread your toes. Feel the weight of your changing body, evenly distributing the weight from the balls of your feet to the fronts of your heels. Contract your front thigh muscles without locking the backs of your knees. Lift your frontal hip points *slightly* (they are the bony points of the pelvis on the front of your body) and drag your tailbone *slightly* toward the floor to level your pelvis. Keep your hips directly over your knees and your knees over your ankles. Draw the sides of your waist up toward your armpits. Broaden your collarbones out toward your shoulders and let your arms hang at your side.

A Few Words About Squats

The design of the human body with a baby in tow is perfect for a squatting stance, so practicing this pose in pregnancy is highly encouraged. As you practice over time, you will find that your body can open more into the squat. From Mountain Pose, start by keeping your feet wider than hips' width and parallel. Exhale. As you bend your knees, come onto the balls of your feet. Your toes may turn out naturally, and you can bring your hands to the floor for support. Keep your toes in the same line as your knees. Stretch your tailbone toward the floor and lengthen the stretch through the top of your head, keeping the spine long. Avoid rounding the spine by letting your heels come off the floor. As you practice over time they will release more toward the floor. If you do not need your hands on the floor for support, bring them into prayer position by pressing your palms evenly into one another, thumbs at your heart.

For assistance you may sit on a block, a stool, or three or four large books. Keep your sits bones on the surface of the stool.

Over time, lower your perch as you grow into the pose. You may also practice this pose with your back against a wall for added support.

To come out of a squat: Bring your hands to the floor, shift your weight slightly forward, and turn your heels out so your feet are more parallel. Come into Uttanasana (Standing Forward Bend) by straightening your legs. Exhale. Release into the Forward Bend, and then come out as instructed for Uttanasana—bending your knees slightly, and bringing your hands onto your thighs for additional support as you roll up to Mountain Pose.

Kegels or Pelvic-Floor Exercises

Kegels, or pelvic-floor exercises, are contractions of the *pubococcygeus muscle*, which is the hammock-like muscle that stretches from the pubic bone to the tailbone, forming the pelvic floor. Conditioning this muscle can provide the strength to make birth easier and help keep your perineum intact (reducing tears and episiotomies). Doing these exercises can also help prevent leaking urine when you sneeze, cough, and laugh hard, or when jumping. Another perk of practicing Kegels (mindfully, of course) is that sexual enjoyment may be enhanced for both partners. By practicing these exercises for the duration of the pregnancy (and your life), you are toning your pelvic floor, which houses your reproductive region, along with about thirty-six pairs of muscles that attach to your pelvis. You can do Kegels just about anytime (while driving, standing in line, watching TV). At a minimum, I recommend doing ten Kegels every time you use the restroom, and when you are pregnant, that's a lot of Kegels! The best way to find this action is to practice stopping the stream while urinating. It is the contracted pubococcygeus muscle that stops the flow. Once you've discovered this muscle, do not stop your urine flow to do the exercise. It is best to do it after you go, perhaps while washing your hands.

Virabhadrasana II: Warrior II

From Tadasana (Mountain Pose), step your feet three-and-a-half to four-and-a-half feet apart. Turn your right foot out 90 degrees so that the heel of your right foot is in line with the arch of your back (left) foot. Keep the ball of your back foot (left foot) on the floor, pick up your heel (left foot) and cut it back left 45 degrees. Engage your thighs by lifting the flesh above your knees. Inhale, lifting your arms up so the palms are parallel to the floor, keeping your shoulders down, away from your ears. Turn your head to look over your right arm. With both legs engaged, exhale and bend the right leg, your knee pointing in the same direction as your toes. Do not let your toes turn in. Eventually the right thigh will be parallel to the floor. Lift your chin slightly up, and be a proud warrior mama! The torso doesn't lean toward the front leg; instead, it is perpendicular to the floor. Start by holding for fifteen to thirty seconds, but work toward holding for one minute to build strength and stamina. Then, bring your feet together again, stand in Tadasana (Mountain Pose), and repeat Warrior II on the opposite side.

Prasarita Padottanasana: Wide-Legged Forward Bend

From Tadasana or Mountain Pose, step your feet three-and-a-half to four-and-a-half feet apart. Your big toes are even with one another, slightly turned in. Evenly press your feet into the floor. Engage your thigh muscles by lifting the flesh above your knees. Inhale and lengthen the spine by lifting the sides of your waist up, toward your armpits. Exhale, keeping the length of your spine long as you bend at the hip crease and come toward the floor, making sure that your hips and heels stay in line with one another. Bring your fingertips onto the floor (or blocks/chair) directly below your shoulders. Breathe deeply as though you were inhaling into the back of your thighs. Keep your head in alignment with your spine, stretching the base of the skull away from your tailbone. Stay in Forward Bend for three to five breaths.

To come up: Lean on the floor or your blocks and narrow your stance by bringing your heels in a few inches, and then toes in a few inches. After you've narrowed your stance, slightly bend your knees, and then press your hands onto the tops of your thighs, using the strength of your arms to help roll up back into Mountain Pose.

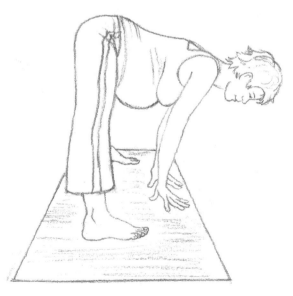

Savasana: Corpse Pose (On Side)

Traditionally, this pose is done flat on the back. However, in pregnancy, it is best to lie on your *left side*, because women in their second and third trimesters may experience a serious condition known as *supine hypotensive syndrome* due to the pressure caused when the mother is in a *supine* position, or lying down on her back. The weight of the uterus, infant, placenta, and amniotic fluids can compress a major vein called the *inferior vena cava*, which can reduce the flow of blood in and out of the heart. When there is pressure on this large vein, your heart rate may decrease and blood pressure may be lowered, causing dizziness, fatigue, nausea, and other ailments. This syndrome can also lead to fetal distress due to a reduction of oxygen to the baby. If you've already had your baby, Savasana can be done lying flat on your back, palms toward the ceiling. Again, bring mindful awareness to your body and breath and discontinue *any* pose that does not feel right.

For Savasana (Corpse Pose), set yourself up on your left side, using pillows and blankets for support as needed to make your Savasana a place of deep peace. Use a firm pillow, a blanket, or a towel under your head, or you may want to use your bottom arm under your head so that it is not jammed under your torso. If you wish, use another pillow between your legs with your top leg slightly forward. Rest your top arm in front of you with your hand on your belly, if you like. Soften your tongue by pressing it hard onto the roof of your mouth, then letting it go, releasing the tension. Unclench your jaw, with your upper and lower teeth not touching one another. Let your body be heavy on the floor. Sink into yourself. Stay in this quiet, restorative pose for at least three to four minutes. If you have time, you may stay as long as ten minutes, or more.

Here is a shortened version of this routine so you can use it as a reference while you practice. Use this quick guide by either propping this book open or photocopying this page to take with you. And if you'd like a more detailed quick-glance guide, you can download it at the website, www.mindfulmotherhood.org.

Mindful-Motherhood Yoga Series:
Quick Glance

Part 1: Sitting Poses

1. **Sukhasana**: Easy Pose (breath awareness)

2. **Upavista Konasana:** Straddled Open-Legs Pose (side stretching)

3. **Baddha Konasana:** Butterfly/Tailor Sitting Pose

4. **Adho Mukha Svanasana:** Downward-Facing Dog

5. **Adho Mukha Virasana:** Child's Pose

Part 2: Standing Poses

1. **Uttanasana:** Standing Forward Bend

2. **Tadasana:** Mountain Pose

3. **Squats and Supported Squats**

4. **Kegels:** Pelvic-Floor Exercises

5. **Virabhadrasana II:** Warrior II

6. **Prasarita Padottanasana:** Wide-Legged Forward Bend

Part 3: Ending Pose

7. **Savasana:** Corpse Pose (on side if pregnant)

5

the three elements
of experience

now that you've got a few practices to start using each day, let's delve more deeply into learning how to observe the different parts of your experiences.

the three elements

One of the participants in our Mindful Motherhood Training for new moms (I'll call her Cindy) told us a story about one of those moments that every mom dreads. At the park one day, she and her husband took their toddler and their four-month-old baby in her stroller to the pond to watch the miniature boats sail. There was a band playing, the sun was shining, a breeze was blowing, kids were laughing and feeding the ducks, vendors were selling hot pretzels and ice cream, and teenagers were roller-blading. It was an all-around lovely day. While she was paying attention to her older child, out of the corner of her eye, Cindy saw the stroller, baby strapped in, rolling toward the pond. Seemingly in slow motion, the stroller rolled right into the pond, baby and all! Luckily the baby only ended up wet and surprised, as she was pulled out of the pond by Cindy's husband. Freeze frame.

This experience contains lots and lots of elements at first glance. There are the sounds of music, kids chatting and laughing, the sparkle of sun reflecting off the water, the feeling of the breeze and the warmth of the sun, the scent of soft pretzels from the cart nearby, the yells of "Hey!" and "Oh my God!" from people who noticed what had happened. For the minute it took for her husband to race to the rescue, Cindy had already had all kinds of thoughts: "How could I have let this happen? I know I set the parking brake on the stroller…or did I? How will I tell people how my baby drowned in a shallow lake in the park? What did they say about baby chest compressions in that infant CPR class!?" Her body tensed up; there was fear and panic. This all became understandably overwhelming quite quickly.

But actually, this experience (and every experience you have) contains three elements: your thoughts, your feelings, and your body's sensations. Even in this complicated moment, there were only three things that were happening in Cindy's experience. She was *thinking:* in this case, trying to figure out how to get to the baby and not leave her toddler alone, and wishing people would get out of the way. She was *feeling:* fearful that her baby was in real danger, shocked, perhaps a little angry, and energized to get to the little one. And, she was *sensing* through her eyes, ears, nose, sense of touch, sense of taste, and body sensations. She took in all the sights and scents around her, the tension, the feelings of wind and sun on her skin, and the sensation of being jostled about by the people in her path.

In every situation you'll encounter as a new mom, whether it is chaotic or mellow, there are three things happening. Examine what's going on for you right now. You are probably having some thoughts, or your mind is focused on reading and digesting this information. You may be having some feelings or emotions. There may be some body sensations, like relaxation, coolness or warmth, or tension. And everything that is happening "outside" of you is being perceived through your senses—the usual five senses of seeing, hearing, touching, smelling, and tasting. There is also a sixth sense that I like to call your *felt sense,* or your gut feelings or overall bodily perception of things (like when the hackles rise on the back of your neck or you feel at home and relaxed). Mindfulness begins with noticing what is happening in these three realms of experience—thinking, feeling, and sensing.

thinking

If you are like me (and like most people I've worked with), your mind chatters constantly. It gives you a running commentary on everything that is occurring. It's almost as though you've got your own personal CNN anchorperson reporting on your life as you are living it. It labels things as good or bad, evaluating each experience. It plans for the future and reflects on the past. It looks for problems or things that are not working or that are out of place, and it tries to solve, fix, or figure them out. It tells stories about how and why things happen in each situation. It categorizes and compares. All of this, whether or not it serves you well, is the realm that we will call *thinking*.

Thinking in and of itself is not a problem. We all have lots and lots of thinking that is positive and helpful. Your thinking may be directed toward solving problems, or appropriately planning for the future, or reflecting on the past. Or your thinking may be simply random—chatting about whatever comes along. Thinking is a useful tool that we humans have been provided with to help figure things out, solve problems, learn from the past, and plan for the future. Thinking is great for things like: "How can I get that peach down from the highest branch?", or "How many diapers will I need over the next month?", or "How can I create a workflow solution that will utilize my department's resources most effectively?" Honest reflection is helpful for processing and learning from situations in the past, for example: "Looking back, I can see that if I had approached my partner with less blame in my tone, things might have gone more smoothly," or "What I think bothers me most about that doctor isn't that I have to wait in the waiting room so long each time, but that he seems too preoccupied to really attend to my pregnancy concerns. I think I'll change doctors."

Unfortunately, though, the internal commentary can get pretty loud. It can take center stage in your experience, relegating everything else—body sensations, your feelings, your environment, sounds and sights, even the person right in front of you—into the background. Your experiences are all filtered through your thinking mind, and your mind can begin to seem a little bit like the guest who won't leave and takes up residence in the living room.

It can become as though your own personal CNN announcer is speaking through a bullhorn. Thinking begins to run the show completely, and rather than engaging directly with what is happening, you are primarily engaged with your story about what is happening. Rather than being engaged with the present moment as it is, you are caught up in the past, in the future, in your evaluations, or in problem solving. Your mind can be like a runaway train from which it's hard to jump off. You can even feel like *you are* your thoughts. I think, therefore I am, right?

feelings

Another part of your experience is emotional. Tune in to what you are feeling right now, emotionally. Sometimes you are feeling discrete emotions, like sadness, joy, guilt, or love. You may be feeling something you can name and you know the origin of—an experience you had or are having with another person, something you read, a memory, or an imagining about the future. Other times, you have more diffuse feelings, like depression, anxiety or agitation, or general contentment. These feelings or moods may not come from any source in particular, but many things might be contributing to the mood—what you've eaten, how the last few days have gone, the season or the time of the month, and so on. And sometimes you have feelings that are pretty hard to put your finger on, that are hard to even name and even harder to find a source for. You might feel an overall sense of stress or a general peacefulness. Most of the time you feel some combination of all of these. This whole realm of being we are going to call *feelings*.

Like thinking, feelings are not problems by themselves. They perform very useful evolutionary functions for you. Fear alerts you to potential dangers in the environment and gets you energized to mobilize a response to the danger. Love, compassion and empathy, and even the grief that accompanies the loss of a loved one ensure that you make strong connections with other people. Shame and guilt, while often harmful, at their roots can help you to maintain ethics and morals as a social being. Even sadness has its upside, helping you to feel for the plight of another, to process a loss or separation, or to recognize and find a resolution to unworkable situations. Happiness, joy, awe, wonder, amazement, surprise—these positive emotions are not just pleasurable, but research shows they are actually linked directly to health and well-being and can serve as buffers or antidotes to more difficult emotions (Folkman and Moskowitz 2000).

The problem occurs when you are either overwhelmed with feelings to the extent that it interferes with your functioning and healthy interactions with others, or when you chronically engage in thought patterns or behaviors to avoid or suppress feelings you perceive as unbearable. Sometimes feelings get so uncomfortable that it becomes hard for you to tolerate your own feelings, or the feelings of those close to you. When pregnant, feelings can be like powerful steam engines, over-whelming and intense, and the ways you usually blow off steam or mellow out (like going for a run or having a drink) might not be possible. When the baby comes, depressed, or anxious, or other overwhelming feelings can be preoccupying, getting in the way of connecting with your baby and enjoying your time together.

sensations

The third realm of experience is sensations. Sensations include everything you sense— what you are seeing, hearing, touching, tasting, or smelling—as well as body sensations. You are probably experiencing some sensations in your body right now. A tightness here, a warm feeling there, an ache or pain, a binding of clothes against skin, or a sort of flow of sensation. You are also always breathing, though most people are rarely consciously aware of that unless they are out of breath. But, when you bring your attention to it, you can feel that you are breathing and may be able to feel your pulse or your heart beating.

Whether they are sights, sounds, tastes, scents, or textures, sensations are typi-cally experienced as (1) pleasant, (2) unpleasant, or (3) neutral—neither pleasant nor unpleasant. Some body sensations, particularly during pregnancy, labor, and early motherhood, are extremely uncomfortable, and some are very pleasurable. You are probably catching on now to what I will say about this. Of course, you want pleasant sensations to stay and uncomfortable sensations to stop, go away, or be beyond your notice. These desires are natural and even useful to a certain extent. It's good that you pull your hand away from a hot stove. But again, like in the realms of thinking and feeling, a lot of unnecessary suffering comes from resisting, strug-gling against, fearing, hating, or attempting to avoid uncomfortable sensations. Terrible scents, awful tastes, or physical pain can be difficult, sometimes even har-rowing experiences. But the unnecessary suffering we often layer on top of the pain is something we can change.

resisting what is

So, if thoughts aren't a problem, feelings aren't a problem, and sensations aren't a problem, what does cause unnecessary suffering? For the most part, it's resisting, rejecting, or struggling against these three elements of your experience. Or, if these elements are pleasant, trying to make them stay can form the basis of your internal battles. Your efforts to stop, resist, or struggle against feelings, or trying to chase after them or make them stay, can form the roots of addictions, bad habits, and negative interpersonal interactions with loved ones, including your children. An example is a plane flight I took a while ago where a woman was attempting to soothe her crying baby.

Now, a crying baby on a plane, especially when it's your child, is not an easy situation by any means. You are tired, cramped, uncomfortable, the noise of the crying seems unbearable, and sometimes your fellow passengers are often not only unhelpful but outwardly antagonistic. I felt a lot of empathy for this woman, having been in similar situations myself.

But watching her, I could see how her resistance to the situation were making it worse than it was by itself. She appeared to have reached her limit of emotional tolerance—of the baby's distress and of her own distress. Her eyes were turned away from the baby's head, she was bouncing the little guy roughly up and down, and if it's possible to yell the sound "Shhhhh," that's what she was doing. Her body was tense, her purse and baby supplies were falling all over the floor, her hair was wild, and her head swung from side to side. In response to my offer to possibly take the baby for a little stroll, she barked, "No, no, you can't do anything. There's nothing to be done."

Now let me be clear here: as a mom, I have certainly reached my limit of emotional tolerance, whether for my own emotions or those of my daughter, and acted in ways I later wished I hadn't. So when I say I had empathy for this woman, I mean not only for her situation but also for her feelings of being overwhelmed. I can imagine what she must have been thinking, the story she was telling herself about this situation: "I've got to make this stop! Please stop—what is wrong? Is he okay?…Oh God, everyone on this plane must hate me. Please make him be quiet! Why didn't I use Benadryl like my sister suggested?" and on and on. But I also knew that if she had been able, even for the briefest moment, to recognize that there was *absolutely no problem* with this baby crying, some of her suffering might have been eased.

How can I say there was no problem with this situation? Such a loud sound in a small cramped space, knowing that her baby was uncomfortable, and knowing that others were also uncomfortable was definitely not preferable. But in truth, the situation was simply that—a loud sound, an uncomfortable baby, some other passengers getting annoyed. That's it. It was resisting the experience, struggling against it, trying to alter, change, stop, or get away from it, and deciding that it was a big problem that should not be happening that was making it worse. In this case, and in many cases, it's our *idea* that difficult thoughts, feelings, and sensations are intolerable and must be suppressed, avoided, or stopped that causes unnecessary suffering, more than the experiences themselves.

With mindful awareness, allowing the situation to be as it was without a lot of judgment about it, approaching the whole thing with compassion and acceptance, she might have still been uncomfortable, but she probably wouldn't have panicked. This is certainly easier said than done. But with practice, over time, this mindset becomes more and more possible.

. . . .

Exercise: Thinking, Feeling, and Doing

This exploration is a practice of observing, noticing, and naming what happens in your experience, one of the foundations of mindful motherhood. There are no right or incorrect answers.

Take out a sheet of paper, turn it so that the long side is horizontal (landscape orientation), and divide it into five equal columns. Now, think of a recent situation that was particularly upsetting, distressing, or difficult. Label the column on the far left "Situation," and write what the situation was (not your story about the situation—just the facts, Ma'am). Label the next column "Thoughts," and write down the thoughts you had about the situation at the time. Label the next column "Feelings," and write what you were feeling at the time (there was likely more than one feeling). Label the next column "Sensations," and write what you were sensing in your body at the time. Label the final column "Behaviors," and write what you did in this situation. (For more guidance, see the forthcoming example.)

Review your table. First, notice how your experience of any situation, however complex, can be reduced to these three elements: your thoughts, your feelings, and your sensations. Is there anything about your experience of this situation that can't be placed into one of these three columns? Remember that, in every situation you encounter, you are actually only able to encounter *your experience* of that situation, which consists of your thoughts, feelings, and sensations. So if someone is screaming at you, your experience is hearing a very loud voice, seeing an angry face, thinking something like, "What the heck is wrong with her?" and perhaps feeling something approaching, "I'm scared." While someone else is certainly involved, it's *your* experience that you have to deal with.

Then, take a second look at the situation itself (the leftmost column). When you look at it discretely, just the facts of the situation without the accompanying thoughts, feelings, or sensations, what is actually happening? Now look at your thoughts in the situation. Are any of them some variation on, "This shouldn't be here"? Are they blaming? Are they self-critical? Do they go far beyond the situation into what it might mean for everything in life? Are they about the past or the future? Are they compassionate?

Next, look at your column of feelings. How much are they in response to the situation itself (column 1) and how much are they a response to your thoughts about the situation (column 2)? For a moment, look at the feelings as though there were no other columns. Do you think some of the feelings are okay, and some are not okay? As you look at each, evaluate whether it's one you feel like you can tolerate. Or is it one that you have a lot of trouble dealing with? For each feeling, consider whether there is some action you usually take when the feeling comes up.

Finally, examine the last column. Did you make a choice about how to behave, or did you feel driven to the behavior? If you made a choice, where in the process did you make it (for instance, right when you became aware of the situation, after your thoughts, after your emotions)? Was your behavior in response to the situation, your thoughts, or your feelings? Are you happy with the behavior? Did it help?

Try doing this exercise again with what is happening for you right now, as you read this book. The left column might say, "I'm reading the book in my rocking chair while nursing," or "I'm reading a book while on the StairMaster at the gym." Then complete the remainder of the columns.

Thinking, Feeling, and Doing

Situation	Thoughts	Feelings	Body Sensations	Behaviors
I got delayed and lost on the way to my daughter's best friend's birthday party and we were late.	I should have left earlier. I should not have gone through the drive-through to get lunch. I should have gotten better directions. I shouldn't be getting upset.	Frustration Shame Guilt Fear (that we would not find it at all) Annoyed Irritated	Tense Hot Rapid breathing Wide eyes Smell of exhaust Bright sunlight Sound of cars	Cursed and said things like, "Come on!" out loud Rushed around trying to find the place

You can use this exercise any time, to help you become aware of the difference between what is happening in your environment, what you are thinking, what you are feeling, and what your sensations are. Rather than trying to change any of them for the time being, the simple process of noticing each of these, disentangling them from one another, and acknowledging them with gentleness, curiosity, and compassion can fundamentally shift the way you deal with all of your experiences during pregnancy, childbirth, and early motherhood. The next chapter tells you more about why.

This is a great exercise to engage in with any situation you find distressing. Notice your sensations, thoughts, and feelings, name them, and then inquire how you responded. This exercise is a process of self-inquiry that can begin to help you notice, in situations that arise in the future, what the actual present-moment facts are, what your thoughts are, what you are feeling, and what you are sensing in your body. Then, in real time, you can better choose a response that makes sense. Just noticing what is happening for you in each situation, rather than being swept up into it without awareness, is a foundation of mindful motherhood.

6

the observing self

in the last chapter you saw that there are three elements of your experience: thoughts, feelings, and sensations. When you think about your experience of who you are, those three elements might seem to cover it. But there is more to who you are, to your experience of being human, than thoughts, feelings, and sensations. There is also an aspect of your being that is *aware* of each of these elements.

At the end of the last chapter, I asked you to reflect on a recent situation that was distressing or difficult and to note your observations about the situation itself, your thoughts, your feelings, your sensations, and your resulting behaviors. What made you capable of reporting on your experience? Who is able to tell us that you were scared, or that you were thinking about calling a friend, or that you felt agitated?

You are able to notice what happened, what you thought about it, how you felt about it, and how your body felt because there is an aspect of your consciousness *in which* all these elements of experience take place.

You have an ever-present internal witness, a part of you that is not identified with your thoughts, not swept away by your feelings, and although it is aware of your sensations, it is not fused with them. It can actually see your thoughts, feelings, and sensations without being caught up in them. There is an aspect of your being that is sometimes called the *observing self*, and it is from this aspect of consciousness that mindfulness springs.

sky mind

One way to describe your awareness is that it is like the sky. Your thoughts, your feelings, your sensations are all like clouds. They arise, they take a form, you can see them, and then they dissipate or pass through. Some days, dark storm clouds fill the entire sky so that all you can see are clouds. A big fight with a friend or your partner, finding out your baby has hoof-and-mouth disease (making you feel like you live in a barnyard somehow), having trouble breastfeeding—all these things can make everything seem pretty dark. Other days, just a few grey clouds take shape and pass through the sky. You didn't get a shower today so you're sweaty and your hair is greasy, or the laundry has piled up and you need to put several loads through. Your pre-pregnancy pants still don't fit when you try them on. You can't figure out how to put the new baby sling on when you need to get out of the house.

Some days there are rainbows—your baby's first smile or first word, the first time your older child says "I love you" to the baby, all those magical moments that make being a mom so much fun. Other days, large, majestic thunderheads make their presence known, cracking open to spill their contents on anyone who happens to be passing by. Your baby is getting a tooth so she's cranky and erupting in screams every few minutes. Your mom gives you an unwelcome piece of parenting advice for the fifth time, and you blow up at her because you think she's saying you aren't doing a good job. You're in your third trimester and you can barely breathe because the baby is squishing your internal organs, then your partner wants you to hurry up so you don't miss the 7 o'clock movie, and you burst into tears.

Sometimes, like winter in the Northeast, bad weather can last for days or even weeks. I had a participant in one of the Mindful Motherhood trainings who experienced *hyperemesis gravidarum*, or constant morning sickness, during her entire pregnancy. Another participant was put on bed rest in week twenty-eight of her pregnancy (yep, that's *twelve weeks* of bed rest). When you are sleep deprived from constantly waking up to pee while you're pregnant, or from feeding the baby every few hours, or through the periods of comforting your babe through teething, or training her to sleep through the night in her own bed, everything can take on a grey overcast that just hangs there.

Maybe your older child gave up naps, or you're pregnant with number two while number one is only six months old. You are extremely tired, and everything you need to do seems overwhelming because you have no energy. You're eating more to compensate for the lack of energy and sleep, so you're gaining weight. Watching your thighs expand is making you depressed. Being tired all the time is affecting your relationship with your spouse. You two are fighting a lot, and everything feels grim. This can last for a long time, and it can look a lot like that yucky grey ice that can cover the ground for months. Sometimes there are even tornados or hurricanes, like divorce, the baby having a serious illness, or dad being deployed to the Middle East.

But all of these weather patterns have something in common. They take place *within* the larger sky. The sky, even when it is covered by a thick fog layer, is always there. It contains all of these weather patterns, but itself remains clear.

Our awareness is sort of like this sky. It's the realm of our experience in which all of our own personal weather patterns arise and pass away. Our thoughts, our feelings, our sensations are like weather patterns. They arise, take a form, stay for a while, but then eventually pass through or dissipate. Sometimes they are big, sometimes small, sometimes beautiful, sometimes ominous—but they always take shape, stay for bit, and then move on.

When you allow the weather patterns to determine who you are, rather than seeing them as contents of your experience that appear and then eventually pass away, you understandably get pretty attached to how these weather patterns appear, how long they stay, and how and when they dissipate. You begin to spend a lot of your energy trying to change or control your experiences, which can be as futile as it would be to try to control or change the weather.

awareness of awareness

Usually as you move through your day, you are engaged with your thoughts, feelings, and sensations, or some combination of the three. So it makes sense that you're going to need to practice locating the place in your being where you're aware of thoughts, feelings, and sensations—the space of awareness in which all of these things are occurring. In a sense, mindfulness is a practice of bringing awareness to awareness itself.

I know—at first this sounds sort of redundant. Or like a Kung Fu movie: "When you become aware of awareness itself, Grasshopper, then you will be a master." But actually, this practice is not abstract at all when you get used to it.

As I've said, the nature of awareness itself *is* naturally mindful, so when you bring attention to the part of you that is aware, you are encountering your natural capacity for mindful awareness (that is, awareness that is in the present moment, nonevaluative, and just notices thoughts, feelings, and sensations with curiosity, as they happen). So this kind of awareness practice does not focus on your breathing, or your body's sensations, or on any of the contents of your experience. Instead, this practice brings to the center of your attention awareness itself.

What does this mean? For a moment, make a mental list of as many contents of your experience as you can. Thoughts, emotions, feelings, sounds, and any other sensations you are aware of. Touch lightly on each one and give it a word or two. "I'm feeling cold." "I'm thinking about dinner." "I'm hearing a bird sing." "I'm seeing a tree."

Now, what is aware of all of that? What part of your consciousness makes it possible to report on all of this? There is an aspect of you that is not a thought, not a feeling, not a sensation, not any combination of any of these. Instead, it is that part of you that is *aware* of all of these things. It is awareness itself.

You are not your thoughts, your feelings, or your sensations.

You are the one who is aware of these thoughts, feelings, and sensations.

Mindful awareness is about changing where you locate yourself. In this analogy, rather than being the clouds, you're actually being the sky. From this perspective, you can see each and every one of your thoughts, feelings, and sensations as things that take place within the vast and limitless space of who you are.

Even if you are looking at a car or a tree, there is an aspect of "you" that is aware that you are seeing. If you are thinking about tomorrow, there is a part of you that can say "Oh, look, there I am thinking about what I'm going to do tomorrow." There is an aspect of your being that is simply aware of everything that appears in your consciousness. Or, perhaps more accurately, awareness is the medium in which everything else happens.

The nature of this awareness is mindfulness. It notices and allows every single thing that enters or leaves your consciousness without comment, evaluation, grasping, or pushing away. If there is any tone at all, it is one of tolerance, allowing, or even mild curiosity. Awareness doesn't try to decide whether or not something should be there; it just notices that it *is* there.

Try this:

Sit in the same way you did in either the body-awareness or breathing practices, or lie down if you think you won't fall asleep. Spend a few minutes practicing breath awareness, which is a great anchor into the present moment. Then practice a few minutes of body awareness, which roots you into the center of your body. Observe your thoughts, feelings, and body sensations, and if it helps to use a word or two to note each sensation, do that. Warmth. Thinking. Aching thigh. Sadness. Heart beating. Itch. Allow each experience to briefly take the center of your attention, kind of like popcorn popping.

Then turn your attention toward the awareness of all these contents—the air in which the popcorn is popping. When I say "turn your attention," I don't really mean to look at it as though you were outside of it. A better way of saying it might be to place your attention in it. Place the center of your being in your awareness, and be aware of that which is aware.

It's a little tricky at first. Another way to do it that has been used throughout the ages is to ask yourself, "Who am I?" You might answer, "A mom, a lawyer, a tennis player, a wife, a good friend, a grocery-store clerk, a movie lover," and so on. Then ask yourself, "Who is aware of being all these things? Who knows all of that?" And once you connect with that space of awareness, notice what it is like. It might feel empty, pure, bare, vast, or simply awake. It can just feel like aliveness. You can even go one step further and inquire who is aware of that aliveness? Who is it that can see that you are aware? In this practice, hang out in that awareness. Let experiences arise and pass away. Center your attention in the awareness itself.

Silence
Be still for just a moment
and let yourself be overtaken
by this thunder
that cannot be heard.
Whether there is a raucous party
raging on inside your head
or all is quiet,
it doesn't matter—
for the Great Silence
is always present,
this awareness
that makes no sound
yet is all music.

You have always
been this song
and the Silence
that birthed it.

—John Astin

Reprinted with permission from John Astin, *Too Intimate for Words* (Santa Cruz, CA: Integrative Arts, 2005).

7

the balloon in the breadbox

when you have a really big thought, feeling, or sensation, it can be like blowing a balloon up in a breadbox. When it blows up completely, it takes up every millimeter of space—there is no room around it at all.

For example, sometimes I think back to when I was still pregnant two weeks after my due date. Around my due date, I'd felt very pregnant, very ready to have the baby, a bit swollen and tired, but still kind of expectantly happy in that way that only happens during pregnancy. As day after day passed with nary a contraction, I became more and more swollen and less and less happy. I had no idea I could get this big, bloated, and exhausted and so, *so* ready for that baby to come. The morning of the fourteenth day after my due date, I woke up, looked down at my belly, and saw a spider's web of stretch marks that had emerged seemingly overnight. Who knew if they'd been there before, but holy cow, were they ever there now.

I immediately started crying uncontrollably. How hideous! They were horrible. I couldn't stand it! Soon I was nearly wailing. I was just bowled over, wishing intensely that things were other than they were—wishing that I'd had the baby, wishing that I did not have stretch marks, hating that I felt so ill-prepared for labor in this whale-like condition. I had pictured myself as a strong, native-like, squatting-natural-childbirth mama who would fiercely attack childbirth as though it were Everest. Now I felt like I could hardly roll over on my side to get out of bed for a tissue. In this moment, the facts of being pregnant, huge, overdue, and with my belly covered with what I thought were disfiguring stretch marks filled my entire experience. It hit me like a freight train. I wanted it all to stop. There was nothing else happening in my experience—I was filled to the brim with struggle.

Then, as had become my habit, I began to notice what was going on for me. I examined my thoughts, my feelings, and my body sensations. I started to chuckle a little in the midst of my tears. I still really disliked it all, no doubt about it. But I found myself able to see my mind struggling so hard against what was happening and how that was causing more distress than all of what was actually happening! Resisting everything that I could not do a single thing about was causing me more upset and more trouble than the actual facts of the situation.

I had to let go. I began to breathe. I lumbered into the living room, now laughing a little at my bear-like gait, and watched a good tearjerker movie. I moved my body around more that day and drank some teas to help start labor. Don't get me wrong—it was not fun. I was still pretty uncomfortable and sad. Mindful awareness and mindful action brought me to a place of presence, acceptance, and a bit of relief, if not happiness and contentment. But for a while there, the balloon of my experience was completely filling the breadbox.

Let's take another example. Say you are home with the baby a few days after giving birth, and your partner has gone out to get some groceries. It's just you and your baby, and secretly, you've been a little apprehensive since coming home from the hospital about taking care of the baby by yourself. What if you drop him? What if he cries uncontrollably? You aren't even sure if you're holding him properly. You're all thumbs when you change his diaper, and he gets cranky and cries. Did you hurt his umbilical spot when taking off the diaper? By the time you get the dang diaper on and the cover figured out, he's in a full wail. So you nurse him.

His latch sends you through the roof, it hurts so much. You hate to admit it, but breastfeeding is not your favorite thing. It's hard for you to take having someone "on you" all the time. And sitting still isn't your forte. The baby is fidgeting and squirming at your breast, and that's making you crazy, so you pop him off and put him on the other side. He won't latch, and he's crying again.

You start to think about your friend Molly, who also just had a baby. She seems like such a natural. She diapers and nurses with such ease. Her baby hardly ever cries. You're afraid that you won't get the hang of being a mother, and you start to cry. You feel inadequate and wonder how all this is affecting your baby. When your partner comes home, both you and the baby are crying uncontrollably.

In this situation, your very natural anxieties about being a new mom have completely filled your consciousness. The difficult aspects of motherhood—the crying, your struggles with breastfeeding, and your own feelings of inadequacy— are looming so large that it's hard to see anything else. Your mind jumps on the emotional bandwagon and starts to add a bunch of unhelpful thoughts into the mix—comparing yourself to your friend Molly, creating globalized fears about the future, blaming you for your failure as a mother to date, yadda yadda yadda. The balloon has completely filled the breadbox.

making the breadbox bigger

Mindfulness practice doesn't stop the balloon from blowing up. It doesn't make you know how to nurse and it doesn't make the stretch marks (or your thoughts and feelings about them) go away. Mindful awareness does not erase, or even always necessarily reduce, your train of thought, your emotions and other states of mind (fear, envy of your friend, anger, frustration, guilt, irritation), or the feelings of physical discomfort (lack of sleep, sore nipples).

Instead, it works toward making the breadbox into the size of a large room. There's enough space around that balloon so that you can both experience it *and* witness it as it's happening. You still have the thoughts, feelings, or sensations. But—and this is key—there are other things happening in your awareness as well.

Remember, you are the one who is *aware* of experiences of distress. And you, as this awareness, are also probably aware of lots of other elements of your experience, including how well you're doing despite not having much experience with babies, how cute your baby is, how sunny it is outside, how much your partner is available and willing to help, how you like the song that is playing on the radio, and that you have friends who are more skilled at this particular stage of motherhood who you can turn to for advice or help. You, as the one who is aware of your internal struggles, can have compassion for this new mama who is trying so hard, who is so tired, and who is so hard on herself. Once you direct your attention to it, there's a whole bunch of space around that balloon that you weren't aware of.

When you've got space around the balloon, when the breadbox gets bigger, you can be aware of all of the other things that are also part of your consciousness, like your goals for how you want to treat yourself or your baby, or positive experiences that are occurring simultaneously. You can be aware of lots of other stuff that would usually be crowded out by the "louder" experiences. And more important, you become aware of the space itself—that deep, quiet ground of being from which everything arises and passes away. While peace of mind can be hard to come by, this space in which all things appear and disappear is by its very nature *already* peaceful, accepting, nonjudging, and allowing, without you having to do anything but rest into it.

What makes the breadbox bigger? When you become *aware* of each of those sensations, each of those thought patterns, each of those feelings and emotions, noticing them just as they are—a big old soup pot of sensations, feelings, and thoughts. You can notice what is actually happening in the situation, putting aside for a moment all your stories about it. What's happening in the previous example is that you are having a tough time breastfeeding and you are a bit apprehensive and not sure about a few things with respect to caring for the baby. That's it.

At that point, you become the one who is aware of all these thoughts, feelings, and sensations, rather than being fused with the thoughts, feelings, and sensations—as though *they* were who you are. They are really just a bunch of ever-changing, temporary thoughts, feelings, and sensations with varying levels of accuracy, intensity, and relevance to the current situation. Some of them are actually completely inaccurate and irrelevant to the current situation.

You can use one of the exercises in the last couple of chapters to bring yourself into noticing your thoughts, feelings, and sensations. Or, you can use the exercise at the end of this chapter, which is designed to help you enlarge the breadbox and strengthen your observing self. What each of those exercises is pointing to is that, even though this moment might feel huge—even though you may feel like you can get no perspective on what's happening, your thoughts like a bullhorn inside your mind, your emotions and sensations taking up every inch of space—the truth is that *there is a whole area of your being that is aware of things other than what's taking center stage at the moment.* You are more than this collection of thoughts, feelings, and sensations. You are the awareness in which they are occurring.

This practice helps you begin to spend more time in your observing self, in that part of you that is aware of everything that is happening. As you begin to spend more time in that witnessing part of your consciousness, you begin to have more space around the balloon. The breadbox begins to get bigger. Your container begins to stretch, just like the belly during pregnancy. But in some ways this container has no limits. As you begin to explore this realm of awareness more, you may find that, like the sky, it's difficult to find any edges.

As your container stretches to be able to hold many experiences at once, you begin to be able to better tolerate distressing or uncomfortable experiences. You can even begin to approach them with curiosity and compassion, because you have more room for them. A big, loud experience still might feel really overwhelming and huge; but even then, there is a little bit of space around it in which you can maneuver. You can be involved in a huge bummer of an experience and still have a fairly good day because that challenging experience doesn't take up every inch of your attention. Other parts of your day get equal playing time.

I can tell the participants in the Mindful Motherhood Training are beginning to catch on when they start saying things like, "I could *see myself* beginning to get really angry. Boy, was I getting steamed!" Initially they might have said, "I was so pissed off, I couldn't stand it." The subtle difference between those two ways of describing the same experience is the difference between being able to stay present, in your body, and connected with your baby during a difficult moment and being swept away into a spiral of anger, resistance, and negative thinking. In the first, you are having an experience and you're aware of it. In the second, the experience has you.

Relocating your center of gravity takes time. It requires repeated experiences of finding yourself in that centered place to begin to get a sense of its flavor and texture, and a feeling for what it might be like to live there more often. I encourage you to do this and the other practices I've described frequently, so that you can explore *being* the awareness in which your experiences are taking place.

Expanding Your Container

The next time you have an experience that you usually don't prefer, see if you can approach it in a new way. Observe the experience just as it is. For example, being too cold is pretty uncomfortable for most people. So, the next time you are too cold, give it five minutes before you turn up the heat, put on a sweater, or go inside.

First observe your body sensations. For a minute, forget about the word "cold" and any thoughts about whether it should or shouldn't be cold. Just feel the sensation we call coldness. If you can, don't tense up

against the cold as you usually would. Try to relax into it. What does cold feel like? Prickly? Brittle? Icy? Bracing? Don't even worry about words too much—just be with the experience itself. Explore it with curiosity.

Don't hold your breath against the sensations you are experiencing. Keep breathing, slow and steady, as you explore the actual sensation you usually call "cold." Try to let thoughts and words fade into the background as you experience the sensations just as they are. Try leaning into it. Play with the experience a little bit. Go into the center of the sensation. Find its edges. Does the experience fill your entire consciousness, or is there a part of your awareness that is outside of the sensation of coldness? Can you find words to describe the sensation aside from "cold"? Name it as many things as you can think of—even nonsense words that sound like good descriptions.

Can you breathe into the sensations and let them be there? If you do have thoughts that intrude into your awareness, can you just let them be there? As you note any emotions that emerge (perhaps anger, fear, or agitation), try to let them be there without doing anything about them. Come out of the cold after a few minutes, but continue to observe the remaining thoughts, feelings, and sensations for a bit. How do they change?

You can try this same approach next time you have any sensations that you would usually draw back from—when you're too hot, you have bodily pain, or the baby is crying, or you get caught in the rain. It's quite amazing how much we can become upset, resistant, or even outraged or panicked when it begins to rain! Instead, see what it's like to just get wet. Observe all your reactions, pleasant and unpleasant. Stretch your container to allow them to be there. You might be surprised!

Deliberately exposing yourself to experiences that are reasonably uncomfortable can help you expand your ability to tolerate moments of discomfort. As you repeatedly and gently *stretch* yourself a little more each time, not only surviving but sometimes even thriving in the face of discomfort, you increase what psychologists call your *self-efficacy*, or your confidence in your capacity to deal with situations. When you know you can tolerate distress, distressing situations that arise actually bother you less, and you become more effective in dealing with them.

You can also find out new things about how you react to challenging situations. For example, many of us meet new situations or even familiar ones with lots of old baggage. When you stretch yourself to be open to an experience you may discover that, in the past, you've met similar situations with expectations that are out of date or inaccurate. For instance, maybe you've always hated having to take the ferry to work because it usually makes you late, takes so much time, and is so crowded. But when your car breaks down, you have to take the ferry for a few days. By opening to it rather than struggling against it, you might find that your feelings have changed. After all, it's been five years since you tried it, and now you surprise yourself by kind of liking it. You've got more patience now, and you find that you're soothed and energized by being on the water. The trip even gives you time to mentally prepare before arriving at work. But if you'd met this experience armored with your old opinions, you may not have realized that there was pleasure to be had in this formerly unpleasant experience.

Letting yourself be with uncomfortable experiences doesn't always result in liking them more, but it does get you more familiar with the territory of discomfort with willingness (as opposed to struggle). When you know the territory better and approach it with willingness, you are better able to navigate it.

8

the train of thought

as you begin to practice mindful awareness (and if you have not tried practicing one of the mindful-awareness exercises in the book or on the website yet, now would be a great time!), you will notice that the thinking, evaluating mind filters all of your experiences. All the ways you react, how you feel, and what you decide to do as a result all are based on how you evaluate the current situation—what meaning you make of it. How you evaluate or make meaning of the current situation is, in turn, highly dependent on your past experiences—what the current situation reminds you of or what it brings up for you. We all make up stories about each experience based on our past experiences and the way we view the world in general, and these stories determine how we think and feel about the situation.

Imagine walking into a coffee shop. You walk in the door and are immediately immersed in the rich smell of fresh coffee. "I like that. I can't wait to get mine." It reminds you of previous cups of coffee, how warm and cozy and good they made you feel. You notice it's very cold in the cafe. "Oh, I hate this. Why do they always have the air conditioning on so high?" Frustration arises, your body tenses up… then you look around. "Wow. Nice, warm wood decorating. I like that." It reminds you of the house you grew up in, and you feel a little more comfort.

Then the line is long. In fact, it's very long and very slow. One person works behind the counter and another worker is reading the paper at a table, apparently on a break. You instantly become agitated. "Why is this line so long? What is that guy doing on a break?"

As the line crawls forward, you get more frustrated. You may even sigh, tap your foot, and comment sarcastically to fellow people waiting. By the time you get the coffee and walk out, you are late, frustrated, annoyed, and basically recall the experience as a negative one.

In this case, your ongoing evaluation of the situation as positive or negative, your conditioning from the past, and perhaps your judgments about the wrongness and injustice of the situation are causing you quite a bit of agitation and frustration. Notice, I don't say the situation *itself* is causing the frustration. Instead, it's the stories you're telling yourself about the situation that cause the emotion. Pema Chodron, meditation teacher and author of the book *When Things Fall Apart*, says, "It isn't the things that are happening to us that cause us to suffer, it's what we say to ourselves about the things that are happening. That's where the suffering comes from" (2003, 1).

The bottom-line evaluation that underlies most of our unnecessary suffering is the thought, "This shouldn't be here." A distant second is, "I like this, and it should be here more."

In the coffee shop example, the beliefs are:

- It shouldn't be this cold.

- This line shouldn't get this long.

- That employee shouldn't be on break.

To a lesser extent agitation is caused by the desire for the pleasurable aspects of experience to happen more, or happen faster. In this case:

- I love that coffee smell.

- I want to be drinking it *now*.

- I like to be on time, I should be on time, and I want to be on time now.

Obviously, evaluation of experience is absolutely normal, necessary, and will continue no matter what you do. Some things are preferable, and some things aren't. But mindful awareness is a way of being in the world in which you are present and aware in each moment, with your thoughts and beliefs being one part of your consciousness, but not completely running the show.

five activities of the thinking mind

Your thinking mind is typically engaged in one or more of five activities.

Survey Says!

First, the thinking mind evaluates whatever is happening. "I love how warm it is today," "I love seeing my midwife; she's the best," "This coffee is too strong," or "I hate the way that woman is looking at me." The mind is very good at rating each experience on a scale from "I like it" to "I don't like it." It's like you've got your very own panel of Olympic judges in your mind, constantly flashing their score cards to rate each situation.

Often, "I like it" automatically means "It's good" and "I don't like it" means "It's bad." And if it's good, you naturally want more of it and you want it to last. If it's bad, you want it to stop and not happen again.

If you tend toward depressive or anxious thinking patterns, you might find that your worrying and judging is often self-directed: "God, my skin is in bad shape," "I'm so behind with everything," "That was a dumb thing to do." Or, your thought patterns might be global: "Why can't I ever get it together?" or "This situation is completely hopeless."

On a general evolutionary level, this rating-things-as-good-or-bad capacity of the mind is really quite useful. In general, when something tastes, smells, or feels good (like sugar or being with a genetically well-matched mate), it's a sign that it *is* good when you're looking at it from the perspective of survival of the species. And, in general, when you perceive something as unpleasant (like rotting food or the feeling of fear when faced by a grizzly bear), it's a sign that it may not support survival or flourishing. However, in this fast-paced, stressful, complex world, our evolutionary tendency to rate things as good or bad has gone a bit haywire. At an emotional level, you can react to things you don't like or don't prefer as things that are threatening your survival. In the same way, you can feel like things you like or prefer are necessary for your survival. So how you rate situations mentally can have significant effects on how you feel and what you do.

Evaluating our experiences is a completely normal task of the thinking mind and can be very useful at times. However, when we make those evaluations the defining factor in our lives, we can run into trouble. Having our peace of mind, our behaviors, and in some cases our very sense of who we are and our value as a person be completely dependent on the ever-changing circumstances of life is a difficult way to live. And one of the primary ways we add to our own stress and difficulty is by habitually evaluating all our experiences and then getting very invested in those evaluations.

Say your ten-month-old baby begins to cry loudly while you are navigating the produce section of the supermarket. You know that she just had a nap because you hung out for an hour in the parking lot of the supermarket waiting for her to wake up. You just changed her diaper, and you fed her just before her nap, so you know she's not wet or hungry. She stops crying when you pick her up. She struggles to get down, wanting to crawl. She doesn't like riding in the baby carrier, and she's now making her protest known throughout the store with her howls of indignation. You really want to finish shopping and get home so you can make dinner. You begin to get angry and embarrassed. You really don't like that she is crying. It falls squarely in the "Not good, and I want it to stop" category.

At this point you have two choices in how you approach the situation. You could decide to resist it—to say "I hate this, I want it to stop, and I'm going to make it stop so I can keep shopping." You might try all kinds of things, and if they don't work, you might get more and more frustrated, embarrassed, and flustered. You might storm out and go home, annoyed for the rest of the evening.

Or you might say to yourself, "The baby is crying. She seems to want to crawl, but that won't work on this dirty floor. Also, I'd really like to finish the shopping." You might stop for a moment and breathe, noticing how your breath is a little faster and your body tense. Given the situation as it is, without any decisions about whether it's good or bad, you might see that you have a lot of choices. For instance, you could stop somewhere and let her crawl around for a while and make dinner late. You could figure out how to carry her. You could give up, go home, and throw that old frozen pizza in the oven. You could borrow some lettuce for a salad from your neighbor. You could let the baby scream and finish your shopping quickly. Still annoyed, you could watch your own irritation and see how it feels. Then you could return to making a decision.

In this case, it is your evaluation of the situation that determines how you react and respond, rather than the situation itself. When you have evaluated the situation as bad, wrong, or something that should not be happening and identify strongly with that evaluation as the "truth," you experience a resulting cascade of difficult emotions, thoughts, and sensations. Then you react. When you meet the situation as it is, you choose the best response available to you given the situation as it is, without a lot of extra stuff piled on.

The Once-and-Future Mom

Second, the thinking mind likes to reflect on the past and plan for the future: "That was some conversation with my partner yesterday, when he said this and I said that and then he said…" "I've got to get to the gym this afternoon." "I've got to pre-enroll my babe in preschool." Often these musings are combined with a layer of evaluation. For example, "I've got to get to the gym this afternoon, and I can't believe I've missed it three days in a row. I'm getting huge! I'll never lose this pregnancy weight." Or, "I can't wait until my brother comes to meet the new baby. That will be so great." Or maybe, "Bouncing that check was a real bummer. Are we ever going to figure out our money stuff?" And, "What if we're not able to get into that preschool…I can't go to the other one every day—it's too far. I should have put our name on the waiting list earlier."

Again, if you tend toward a pattern of negative thinking, you might tend to generalize about the past or preferentially remember negative emotional events. For example, you might still be holding it against yourself that you never finished that graduate degree or that you once dropped the baby on his head on the stone-tile kitchen floor. (This actually happened to a friend of mine. Don't worry—the baby was fine.)

It can also be a habit to frequently anticipate catastrophe: "My baby hasn't started saying words yet and Lida's son is two months younger and already has. What if my boy has a learning disability?" Or, "What if we can't pay our mortgage?" And even, "I just know something is going to go wrong."

One way mindful awareness is different from the thinking mind is that it spends all of its time in the present moment. I'll talk a lot more about this later, but for now, begin to notice how much of your thinking is about the past or the future. Don't try to change it, just notice it.

What's Not Working

In addition to evaluating, reflecting, and planning, our thinking mind wants to solve problems. It scans the environment for potential problems and tries to come up with solutions.

Remember those magazines you got as a kid that had a picture of a town, for example, and asked you to find all the things that did not belong, such as someone riding a bicycle upside down or a house without a roof?

Often your thinking mind feels automatically pulled toward things that are out of place or situations that need resolving. The mind has a tendency to direct attention toward things that are broken, that are not working well, that seem to need attention.

So, say that you're having a lovely time at the playground with your baby daughter. Things in your internal experience are quiet. So, your mind does its thing and begins to scan your experience for something that is not working, that's out of place. Hmm, nothing is not working or out of place there at the playground. So, the thinking mind widens its search parameters to include the past and the future. Bingo! Suddenly you remember something that happened at work yesterday. It didn't seem too bad at the time, but it may pose a problem, so you get on your cell phone to deal with it while you're pushing the baby on the swing. Suddenly you are neither here nor there. Your thoughts, feelings, and sensations have to do with what happened yesterday and what might happen tomorrow, rather than what is happening in the present moment. You're worried about what happened in the past and what might happen in the future while you miss out on the pleasure of the moment.

Colleagues of mine, Rick Hanson and Richard Mendius, write about why this is the case (2007). If you think about how we've evolved as a species, about what kinds of traits survived best over the millennia, do you think it was the little furry precursors to humans who were pretty chilled out and mellow who survived and therefore successfully reproduced?

As Rick and Rick point out, it probably wasn't the especially easygoing little guys who survived. The ones who made it were those who were hypervigilant, who really knew how to look for danger, for threat, for what was not working, for what to *avoid*. So, it stands to reason that a great number of us are hardwired to look for problems and to spend our time striving mightily to solve them. Nowadays, according to the Ricks, when there are so many fewer life-threatening dangers, we've transferred that tendency toward hypervigilance to our everyday lives. Now, most of us certainly face very conceptually complicated situations every day, but very few are life threatening. Because of this, we actually have to work hard to *train* ourselves to relax, to look for what *is* working, to be in the moment, to be present.

The Storytelling Mind

Fourth, your thinking mind also likes to create stories about what is happening. It tries to make meaning of each situation, making guesses about why your partner is late, why your baby isn't sleeping through the night, what might be wrong with the baby that keeps getting the hiccups in your belly, what it will mean about you if you ask for pain medication during childbirth, what it means that your mother-in-law did not come to visit you in the hospital, and so on. Your mind has a story for everything, from the most simple ("I'm hungry, and I need to eat"), to very complex stories about why, what, who, and how things happen.

Our stories, at best, vary in their degree of accuracy. In fact, research shows that our memories about events in the past and how we felt about them at the time are often mistaken (Hassan 2006). All experiences, current and past, are being filtered through your perceptions, your biases, and your expectations and then your memories of them altered by the meaning you make of them as time passes. Even in the present, many of your thoughts are just stories—what someone is thinking when they look at you, what it means that your partner didn't take out the garbage again, what you imagine when someone is late again or doesn't call you back.

In other words, *your thoughts are not facts*. They are ways that you are making meaning out of what you're perceiving. And because thoughts are not facts, you don't have to believe every thought you have. You can begin to approach each thought as what scientists call a *working hypothesis,* or the best guess you can make with the information available to you at the time. Working hypotheses are not to be blindly believed; they are meant to be tested to see if they are true, to be held lightly and to be open to revision if information that contradicts them comes along.

When approached in this way, your stories about what is happening begin to gradually lose their hold on you. You are able to say, "I was wondering why you didn't come to visit me in the hospital after the baby was born" and really listen for the answer, rather than spitting, "I can't believe you didn't come to visit me in the hospital!" Your thought process might become, "I'll have to ask her about that," rather than, "She doesn't care about me, and she never has!" Even if you have the latter thought, which you very well may, you can look at it and say, "Wow, her not coming to the hospital made me think she doesn't care," rather than being completely fused with the belief, "She doesn't care."

The Comparing and Categorizing Mind

Finally, the mind likes to compare, contrast, and categorize information, most often placing it into the big bins of "Good, I like it, I want more of it", and "Bad, I don't like it, it shouldn't be here." But there are other bins as well. Your mind, for the sake of efficiency, decides how whole groups of things are and fits your new experiences into one of those groups. This is fine when you're talking about the difference between Washington apples (red and sweet) and Granny Smiths (crunchy and tart). But when you're making assumptions about more complex situations or about people, categorizing can keep you from seeing what's right in front of you. You can have an overarching belief that women who are nursing their babies when you had to bottle feed are judgmental and superior. You can believe that people who share a family bed are too loose and undisciplined, or those who do sleep training by six weeks are cold and unfeeling. These assumptions keep you from seeing how things really are, in all their rich variability, in each new situation.

Finally, the mind likes to compare. It looks for differences, and if it identifies them, it evaluates which variation is preferable or problematic. This is just a built-in function of the mind—it's not good or bad. The problem comes when we believe these comparisons completely and then react to them emotionally and with our behavior. You might compare your appearance against someone else's ("How did she lose all her pregnancy weight in four weeks?"). You might compare another mom's performance to yours ("Can't she see how she's spoiling her baby?"). Or, one of the mind's favorite activities, you might create an imaginary, unachievable ideal and compare yourself against that ("I should have a conflict-free marriage, be content and fulfilled as a stay-at-home mom, be cheerful and sexually vibrant, and not worry about money"). The comparison function of the mind is useful, but if you can recognize it as a *habit of mind* rather than *the truth*, you can let those thoughts pass right through rather than grabbing hold of them.

Even if you agree with what I'm saying about this, your mind will continue to categorize and compare. That's just what it does. If you can *see* it, rather than *be* it, you've got the key to some liberation from the thinking mind.

getting across the railroad tracks

Let's say you have a beautiful baby girl who happily nurses and coos and makes your heart melt. You, your partner, and your child are living in a bubble of bliss. You go for walks together, sleep together, and you and your partner stare at the baby for hours. Life as a mom is better than you ever imagined.

Then the time comes for your partner to go back to work, and you are alone with the baby all day. Finding time to shower and eat is difficult, never mind e-mailing, calling friends, getting the house picked up, or doing a little work. Your days are all about nursing, changing diapers, and rocking and holding the baby. You start to feel isolated and lonely.

When your partner gets home from work, she's tired and needs to regroup. All you want is for her to take the baby and give you a break. You think that she's not helping out enough, and you start getting resentful. "Shouldn't she want to spend time with her own child? Didn't she miss her?" You're feeling underappreciated. You are overwhelmed by and feel guilty about thoughts of wanting your old life back. You and your partner are starting to snap and fight, and you never used to before the baby. You're miserable.

In this situation, having some internal struggle, some sadness and anger, and some negative thinking is absolutely normal, natural, and understandable. But the misery comes from your response to *how your mind rates each event*. Cooing, nursing, walks, cuddling…these are all good. Not having a shower, not talking to friends, feelings of isolation…these are all bad. Your partner's lack of involvement…bad. Your own disappointment and wishing to have your old life back… bad. Fighting with your partner…bad.

While reading that story, did you make judgments as a reader about whether the elements of this situation are indeed good or bad and how good or bad each one is? (Isn't it amazing how automatic it is?) For a moment, suspend the need to decide whether the elements of this situation are good or bad and just look at each as it is.

Cooing. Nursing easily. Taking family walks. Difficulty connecting with friends. A tired partner who isn't changing diapers or holding the baby. Bickering with that partner. These things are all happening. They are exactly what is happening, and nothing else. When viewed without judgment, each of these events becomes something that could be approached in many different ways.

If you were in this situation, your judging mind might say, "Why the heck can't my partner help me more? I know what that means—it means she doesn't care about me or the baby. She broke her promise, and I knew she would." However, with mindful awareness, the same situation can become, "I feel tired. I would like help. I wish my partner would help out more." Not bad. Not good. Just what is. No one is right. No one is wrong.

Addressing the situation with mindful awareness is so much easier and more effective than trying to address the first, judging-mind perception of the situation. It's also more accurate, takes less time to resolve, and frees up a lot of energy to be with your baby and notice the things that are going well, in addition to those that are not working as well.

don't believe everything you think

You will not be able to wrestle down the evaluating, planning, reflecting, strategizing, comparing, and categorizing mind. It's not as though you will be able to stop your own personal CNN announcer from constantly commenting on your experience, reporting all the horrible parts of your history, or sensationalizing what is to come. But when you bring mindful awareness to your thinking mind, you *can* make that CNN anchorperson more like the news bar that runs across the bottom of the CNN screen. I'm talking about that ticker tape that quietly slides along telling you all kinds of information, some relevant and interesting and some not.

It's like demoting the thought announcer with the bullhorn to be more like a radio announcer, playing more softly on a radio in the background. If you are listening for a weather or traffic report, you can attend to it. Otherwise, much of the information is just commentary—some of it useful and some not.

You don't need to believe everything you think. As you learned in chapter 5, you have emotions and at least five other senses to provide information. But you also have your awareness. You can cultivate the ability to respond to each situation exactly as it is, rather than based on the story you are telling yourself about it. This ability invariably leads to making choices that are wiser, yield better results, and reflect who you are and what you believe in more accurately.

Sylvia Boorstein, meditation teacher and author of *Happiness Is an Inside Job: Practicing for a Joyful Life* (2007), says that mindfulness is the habit of seeing things in an uncomplicated way. What mindful awareness is, more than anything, is being able to be present and aware for each experience as it arises, and meeting it with friendliness, toward the experience and toward yourself. This holds true for how you approach your thinking.

Thinking is just another experience. You may become aware of *ruminating*, or really loud self-critical, evaluative, and striving mind-chatter. In that moment, you are being mindful. Why? Because you are aware of the rumination. This means that something besides the rumination is happening. *You* are observing it. You might be observing the ways that your thinking mind is trying to suppress or get away from an uncomfortable sensation. Your observation of that process *is* mindfulness.

thank-you mind

If you are like me and a lot of moms I've worked with, your mind is waiting for you when you wake up with a whole list of things it wants you to attend to—right now, if you please. This makes waking up a perfect time to spend a few minutes on mindful-awareness practice—in effect, saying to your mind, "Thank you for your help, and I'm sure I'll want to consult with you throughout the day. But you are only one source of information for me. *I* am the one who is aware of *you*." This can set the tone for the day, clarifying the chain of command, so to speak.

> **Spend a few moments doing awareness of your breathing and body sensations (see chapter 2 or chapter 3). Notice your breathing. See if you can locate the center of your being as that which is aware of breathing—the one who is breathing. Spend a few more moments being the one who is aware of your body and its sensations, bringing the center of your awareness into your belly, and having it radiate outward from there. Next, rather than feeling like you are your thoughts, be the one who is aware of your train of thought. Watch those railcars go by, one**

by one, and don't jump on any one of them at the moment. (You can always come back to one later, if you choose.)

If your mind really struggles for dominance, try directing some very gentle, compassionate, loving attention toward your thinking. Send it some truly appreciative thanks for working so hard. Feel, if you can, the awe, wonder, and reverence the mind deserves for all it can do. It's really pretty amazing.

Have compassion for all the ways your mind twists itself into tangles, how it gets confused, and how it can get pretty miserable all on its own. Have sympathy for how hard it is on itself, how impatient it gets with uncertainty or not knowing (in fact, very creative places to be). Have compassion for how upset your mind gets when it thinks it's missed something or made the wrong decision. Try to be compassionate when your mind thinks there is only one right decision, and if it could only think hard enough, it could find the answer.

Give your mind permission not to work so hard. Relieve it from having to be in charge of everything all the time. Tell your mind it is no longer being asked to figure things out that are not amenable to being figured out. You are now going to distribute the tasks of living more equally to all the parts of your being. Kindly and gently let your mind know that it is being invited to take a break from time to time, that it can rest. Give it a more realistic expectation, such as "Mind, I expect you to offer your input as one of many sources of information I have. Take a load off, Mind."

Sit and breathe for several minutes.

Let the mind do exactly what it does—whether it is relatively silent at the moment or chattering like a monkey.

Let your body and its sensations be exactly as they are.

Let your feelings and emotions be as they are.

Be still.

Be.

SECTION 2

The Qualities of Mindful Motherhood

9

how is mindfulness different?

in one Mindful Motherhood training session, a woman I'll call Rachel, balancing her baby on her knee, said, "Okay, not to be trouble, but I watch myself all the time. That's my problem! I'm constantly watching myself. I notice everything that happens, I'm always thinking about what is happening, reflecting, observing, noticing...too much! I beat myself up and second-guess myself all the time. It doesn't help me at all—it's neurotic! How is this different?" What a great question!

In general, mindfulness is being aware and present for all of our experiences as they unfold throughout our days. In response to Rachel's question, it's not "thinking about what is happening." It's *being aware* of what is happening in the present moment. These are two very different things. What makes them different?

mindfulness is not self-control

Using other methods, you can learn coping skills that focus on changing the way you think about situations, stopping thoughts that are not healthy for you, or distracting yourself from troubling emotions or body sensations. And these are all possible, and perhaps called for in some situations. But I find them limited, particularly in pregnancy and early motherhood.

This distinction is essential.

> **Mindfulness is not a method for suppressing or controlling thoughts, emotions, or body sensations.**

Why do I think mindfulness can be more helpful than attempts at cognitive control during pregnancy and early motherhood? Because some thinking patterns, emotions, and body sensations can be like unstoppable freight trains during this period of time. Attempts to change them, make them stop, or shove them underground by suppressing them can be not only unsuccessful but counterproductive.

For example, when Janice was in full-blown labor it completely overwhelmed her. She didn't want her husband to touch her or her mother to be in the room. She tensed her entire body and gritted her teeth through each contraction, no matter what the nurse suggested. Janice would not use any of the techniques she learned in birthing class. She was scared and became fixated on getting her next dose of painkiller through her epidural. Transition was a nightmare. She hid herself in the bathroom and refused to have the baby, moaning, "Make it stop, make it stop!" When it came time to push, she said she just couldn't do it. Nothing her husband or mother said helped. The midwife finally had to hold Janice's face and tell her if she wanted to end the pain and have her baby she needed to bear down and push. Now.

I'm not saying that Janice was doing anything "wrong." While I think that mindful awareness can help tremendously in childbirth, I also strongly believe that childbirth is a unique situation. In some ways, all bets are off—nearly anything goes when you're giving birth. Reading this, most of us can feel a lot of compassion for Janice. But from that place of compassion, it's clear from the outside how Janice's state of mind was making labor even more difficult for her.

In fact, Janice's resistance to what was happening, her attempts to stop or avoid the pain, exacerbated it. She got locked into resisting her experience, digging her heels in. Because her pain, her fear, and her thoughts "I can't do this" and "Make it stop" were taking up every inch of her consciousness, the only thing she experienced was anger, fear, pain, and resistance.

While this is an extreme example, it applies just as well to all the miniature freight-train experiences you'll encounter during pregnancy and early motherhood (and beyond!). This period is a very special time, as you know, but it contains some unique challenges (as you're undoubtedly also becoming aware of). There may be a lot of irritation, or depressive moments that can come with lack of sleep in the first several weeks of the baby's life. There can be physical pain and discomfort of all sorts. Most couples experience ups and downs in their relationship with each other and with older children as everyone tries to get their sea legs in this very new way of life. All kinds of powerful thoughts, feelings, and sensations are part of the package with pregnancy, childbirth, and early motherhood, and attempts to control or avoid them only add to the struggle and distress of those moments.

In some ways, thoughts, feelings, and sensations are like the waves in the ocean. And trying to alter or stop them is like trying to stop the waves from endlessly rolling in. Sometimes, in order to behave in line with your values and goals, you may try to control or clamp down on your thoughts and feelings. This is sometimes possible, but not always, and typically not for extended periods. Attempting to control, change, or suppress emotions, thoughts, and sensations can be like treading water—it's time limited. You can do it, but for only so long. When you get tired, hungry, overwhelmed, or flooded with hormones, it's easy to be swept under, only to have to struggle your way back up again.

This is not to say that you should never attempt to reframe a situation more positively or calm an internal sense of panic through counting to ten and breathing. By all means, if you can avert an emotional downward spiral by looking for the positive in a situation rather than the negative, forcefully stopping yourself from sinking into a self-critical tirade, or removing yourself from an unhappy situation, do so. These kinds of skills are some of the essential building blocks of emotional health.

But mindfulness is an essentially different approach to your experiences, and it's an essential tool to have in your toolbox for those times when thoughts, feelings, sensations, and situations can't be changed or avoided. Take the example of the crying baby on an airplane from chapter 5. This is a situation that is impossible to get out of, in which it would be difficult to suppress or change your thoughts and feelings, and the sensations involved are not under your control (like the baby crying, the plane being hot and stuffy, and other passengers' looks and sighs). In this situation, it's great to have a way to approach experience that allows the experience to be there exactly as it is *and* helps you feel less distressed and make conscious choices about how to respond.

the freedom to choose

Mindfulness is great in situations where you don't want to change anything about what is happening, but it's still distressing, and you'd like to be able to remain present and able to function in the face of that distress. For example, you may need to interview for a job that you want a lot, and you feel quite intimidated and nervous. You might be called upon to speak publicly about something you are passionate about and really want to do it, but you're also seized by stage fright. You may have anxiety about flying but really want to visit your grandmother who lives on the opposite side of the country. Or, you might have a baby who is crying due to stomach pain or colic, and while you may not be able to change the situation, you really want to be able to remain present, aware, and nurturing in those moments.

We all have our favorite coping strategies to deal with situations like this— some healthy and some not as healthy. Some of these are calling a friend, taking a walk, taking some time out for ourselves, distracting ourselves, trying to ignore the experience or pushing it down in our consciousness, drinking alcohol, nitpicking at our partner, playing computer solitaire, reading, or working. None of these, in moderation, is a serious problem. It's fine to distract yourself with a funny movie, go to the gym to work off an angry moment, relax with a game of solitaire, or get involved with a big project.

The problem comes in when you feel *incapable* of facing your experiences, and feel *compelled* to engage in behaviors that get you away from them. Or when you feel distressed each time things don't go the way you'd planned, or an unexpected obstacle presents itself (in other words, attempts to control situations have failed). You can even get in trouble in response to pleasant compelling experiences, like getting positive feedback from others on your work or your appearance, when you grab on tight to them to make them stay or make their presence necessary for your happiness.

More suffering is created when difficulty meeting your experiences as they are leads you to act in ways that are not in alignment with your values and goals. In other words, difficulty facing your present-moment experience can prevent you from acting like the mom you want to be, whether that is something as subtle as breaking contact with your baby because it's hard to tolerate her crying, or getting tense and irritable, or being so stressed during pregnancy that you are not thriving nutritionally or getting enough rest. It can even extend to more extreme reactions, like using substances or shouting at or being physically rough with your child.

The idea with mindful awareness is not necessarily to calm down, to change your essential emotions or to provide distraction. Mindful awareness is not directed toward changing your experiences (they are always changing by themselves anyway!). But, it may help to suppress or alter *behavior* or *actions* that are not in line with the kind of mother you want to be.

The goal of mindful motherhood is not to come up with new and better ways to change your experiences, but instead to cultivate a way of staying present, aware, and connected with your baby *while you are having your experiences*, no matter what they are. This is the focus of mindful motherhood: being able to have your feelings while still behaving in ways that are congruent with your values and goals—who you are and how you want to be.

mindfulness: changing how you relate to your experiences

This is a very important distinction, one I want to make sure you understand. Mindfulness is different from other coping techniques in that the goal is not to change "faulty thinking," to alter what you are feeling, or to change the situation you are in. Mindfulness is not directed toward changing the contents of your experience (thoughts, feelings, sensations), though this can and often does happen.

> **Mindfulness is changing how you relate to your thoughts, feelings, and sensations.**

It's approaching your thoughts, feelings, sensations, and the contents of your environment (your baby, your house, your partner, your work, all of it) by:
Paying attention to them
  in the present moment
    without judging them as good or bad;
      just letting them be as they are,
        when possible, approaching them with curiosity and compassion,
          letting them move through as they will,
            breathing the whole time,
              without having to do anything about them
                but taking skillful and intentional action when called for.

Notice that this way of approaching your thoughts, feelings, and sensations turns out to be a pretty good way of approaching not only your experiences, but your child as well—whether still cooking in the belly, a baby, a toddler, a kid, or a teenager.

Sometimes when I'm teaching a Mindful Motherhood class, students come in and say, "I tried mindfulness, but it didn't work."

"What does 'not working' mean?" I ask.

"Well, I didn't feel any better at all! In fact, I felt worse!"

"Were you aware of what you were thinking and feeling?" I ask.

"Well, yes."

"Did you breathe? Was your behavior in alignment with how you want to be as a mom? Did you stay connected with your baby?"

"Ummm...Yeah, pretty much."

"That's mindful motherhood! You did it!"

It's like what one of my colleagues, Zindel Segal, shared about a participant in the Mindfulness-Based Cognitive Therapy groups he and his colleagues developed for people recovering from depression (Segal, Williams, and Teasdale 2002). This participant said, "I'm still depressed sometimes, but I'm just not letting it make me miserable anymore!"

The great news is that, although mindful motherhood is not aimed at changing the contents of your experience, making them all pleasurable, or getting rid of the unpleasant contents (I'd be a millionaire if I'd discovered that secret!), it often does have the effect of cultivating a much more stable peace of being that is not dependent on circumstances.

With mindfulness, even when you're feeling sadness, fear, anger, or guilt, you have an increasing capacity to remain present, to stay connected with your baby, to be able to set nurturing limits (for both yourself and your babe), and to respond to what is actually happening rather than reacting to your story about what is happening. You are less likely to translate those pure, normal, and natural emotions into more chronic experiences of depression, anxiety, rage, or shame. More and more, you are able to act in alignment with your values and your goals to be the kind of mother you want to be.

the way the sail takes the wind

Mindful awareness, as you are probably beginning to notice if you've been doing the practices at the end of the preceding chapters, has some qualities that are very different from your usual way of being. Mindful awareness is not only awareness and presence; it is a certain *kind* of awareness and presence. Mindful awareness is not only attending to our experiences as they arise, being aware of them, noticing them and observing them. Mindful awareness is being aware of our thoughts, feelings, and sensations *in a particular way*—from a specific frame of reference and with a certain attitude.

The word "attitude" was originally a nautical term, meaning the way the sail takes the wind. So when I say attitude, I don't mean looking on the bright side or being more optimistic. I mean approaching all of our experiences as moms, whether pleasant or unpleasant, easy or difficult, big or small, by meeting them exactly as they are, without resistance or struggle, not trying to make them different, allowing them to be as they are, and over time, approaching them with curiosity and compassion. It's meeting our experiences without judging them. With acceptance. As a sail meets the wind.

Earlier, I talked about mindful-awareness practice as exploring or spending more time in a territory that you might be unfamiliar with. If you were an explorer and you were looking for a territory that you hadn't been to before or hadn't spent much time in, before you could explore it you'd need to find it. If I told you, "You'll know it when you get there, because there will be a bunch of sand dunes, a stand of palm trees, a big river, and you'll see a bunch of pyramids in the west," you'd have an easier time finding it.

In the next chapters, I talk about some of the attitudes that characterize mindful awareness. Just like mindful awareness, these qualities are attitudes that you can cultivate. You can *practice* being more accepting, engaging in less striving for things to be other than they are, being more present-moment focused, less judgmental, more curious, or compassionate. But these attitudes are also like landmarks. You can spend more time in the aspects of yourself that are *already* accepting, nonjudging, nonstriving, curious, and compassionate. Mindful awareness, by its very nature, is these things. So when you encounter these attitudes toward your experience, you'll know that you are in the territory of mindful awareness.

10

acceptance: meeting motherhood as it is

quite often, your thinking mind can be ticking along in a very positive manner: "Okay, I feel great. I'm so ready for this day! My baby is happy, I'm so glad I'll be seeing my good friend this afternoon, and things couldn't be better." Your mind is evaluating the present circumstances as "good," it's scanned the environment and not found any problems to solve, and it's currently relatively settled with the past and is looking forward to the future. There are those times when everything lines up beautifully, and these times are great blessings. It's relatively easy to practice acceptance during these moments.

The only problem is that you can spend a lot of time and energy striving to get everything to line up beautifully so that you can experience this pleasure and peace of mind. It's a full-time job. Indeed, you can spend most of your time and energy trying to get your ducks in a row, to get it all together, so that *then* you can relax and be happy. In fact, most of us do spend quite a bit of time trying to get everything running smoothly. When you really think about it though, this endeavor can become a treadmill. It can begin to feel a bit like a hamster wheel—you run and run, but you never arrive.

Your happiness and peace of mind can become entirely conditional on the circumstances—in other words, whether or not you have peace of mind depends on how things are going in your life. And, because your peace of mind is dependent on these factors, you understandably spend quite a bit of time trying to control or change your circumstances. And when things don't fall into line, you might block out or numb yourself against what's not working. Mindfulness is an entirely different approach to life that works toward cultivating a certain sense of stability and peace *no matter what the circumstances are.*

this shouldn't be here

Most of our unnecessary suffering comes from wanting things to be other than they are. Wait a minute, you say. That can't be true. My wanting things to be other than they are is what motivates me to improve them! If I didn't dislike my house being dirty, I'd never clean it!

There may be some truth to this point. But from the perspective of mindful awareness, if your peace of mind *depends* on your house being clean and you simply don't have time or energy to clean it for a few days, then your peace of mind is out the window! Having your contentment be based on so many ever-changing circumstances is a losing proposition.

But, you might argue, what about a battered woman? Shouldn't she want things to be other than they are? If your child is sick, isn't it totally normal to want things to be other than they are? Indeed, there are certainly circumstances that can cause a lot of pain and grief, and not liking them and wishing they were not there is completely understandable. The kind of pain and grief that come from seeing your baby ill, losing something or someone important to you, or being treated badly by another are not what I mean when I say "unnecessary suffering."

There is pain that is a part of being alive, and accepting that rather than resisting it is part of what mindful motherhood is all about. We all run into difficulties, small and large, in the usual course of each day, and we understandably experience painful emotions in reaction to those situations. Your baby will get sick from time to time, you may experience the loss of loved ones or conflict with them, you may find yourself in sticky political situations at work, or experience difficult family dynamics. And taking action to alleviate or prevent pain is a worthy pursuit if approached intentionally and skillfully.

When I say *unnecessary suffering,* I'm talking about the unnecessary layers of worry, rumination, struggle, and difficulty we put on top of the original problem. Sylvia Boorstein, beloved meditation teacher, mother, and grandmother who wrote the foreword to this book, says that "suffering is the extra tension created in the mind when it struggles" (2005, 1).

So when, in response to any experience you encounter, you:

resist it	grasp at it
hate it	make it necessary for your happiness
try to get away from it	try to get more of it
blame others for it	blame yourself for it
try to find reasons for it	get global and hopeless about it
tell yourself long stories about it	suppress, avoid, or distract yourself from it

which most of us do quite naturally and frequently, you may be adding layers of unnecessary suffering, making difficult experiences harder and even making pleasant experiences less pleasurable. Like when your baby finally gets down for a nap after a long struggle, and you say to yourself, "God, I hope this lasts more than a half hour," instead of allowing that sweet relief to suffuse every part of your body.

Pema Chodron, another wonderfully clear and compassionate meditation teacher and author of *Comfortable with Uncertainty* (2008), calls it the "tendency to make matters worse." Even if you have a genuinely great loss, she says, "The root of it turning into debilitating suffering is what you do with that, how you spin off from that" (2007a, 1).

Let's use an example. I had a student recently whose car was stolen. She called me to cancel an appointment we had together and was understandably quite shaken and upset. She was on her way to the police station to make a report, and said she'd see me the following week. When I saw her, she told me how it had felt to find the broken glass on the street, realize the car had been stolen, and figure out what to do next. I asked her how she felt now. She said, "Oh, it's a real bummer, but it will be fine. I'll have to use public transportation and can borrow a car from time to time from a family member until I can afford a new one, which is a hassle. But I'll work it out. I didn't have insurance and still have to pay off the old car before I can buy a new one, but what can I do? Now I'm focused on getting back to my patients." In our supervisory sessions from then on, I don't think she mentioned it once.

In contrast, a coworker of mine a while back fell on a staircase and twisted her ankle. It turned out to be a fairly bad sprain, and it was more difficult to get around than usual. She could still drive, but she had to find closer places to park and had difficulty getting from place to place. It was a big inconvenience and physically uncomfortable. But in contrast to the student in the preceding story, this person made the sprained ankle a central part of her life for the weeks she was inconvenienced and then for several weeks afterward.

She was angry at herself for falling and berated herself about it vocally. She was disappointed with her treating physicians who could not find a better solution to her discomfort and for whom she had to wait in the waiting room for too long at her appointments. Being slowed down in getting from place to place was making her work life less productive, and this was unacceptable to her. She couldn't go running as she usually did and was worried about getting out of shape and gaining weight. She struggled against the discomfort itself, lifting the leg to be elevated with a loud grunt when she sat down and shaking her head disgustedly. She often said things like, "I'll have to limp over there to do it," or "Clumsy and slow, that's me." Even weeks later, she'd refer back to the event as a major landmark in her life. For example, she'd share memories of an event with coworkers and say, "Oh, right— that was before the sprain."

What is the difference between these two situations? One could argue which one was worse, the sprained ankle or the stolen car, and therefore caused more suffering. But I would suggest that the difference in suffering between these two women came primarily from one thing: each person's ability to meet and accept the situation as what was happening rather than spending so much energy resisting or struggling against it.

The source of most of our unnecessary suffering is the following statement:

This shouldn't be here.

The idea that the way things *are* is not the way they *should be* causes people, moms in particular, a lot of unnecessary suffering. An idea that places a distant second and causes most of the remainder of our unnecessary suffering is the statement:

> **Something should be here, and until it is here,
> I can't be happy.**

Most of our psychological, emotional, and interpersonal difficulties are not in fact caused by our circumstances (though some certainly are). Instead, these difficulties find their roots in our struggle against things as they are. Addictions are overuse of substances to change how we feel. Most fights with loved ones or partners are rooted in wanting the other person to act differently or *be* different. Stress most often comes from resisting things the way they are.

this is, as it is

Mindfulness is grounded in the awareness that *things are always exactly as they are.* This may seem very obvious or even philosophical. But when you take some time to explore the idea, it becomes clear that a whole lot of struggling in life comes from not settling in to this fact. Things are the way they are.

Acceptance, the way I use it here, is not approval. It does not mean you decide to *like* the way things are or that you accept the situation in the sense of it being good, right, or even okay. It means that you recognize that things are they way they are, and no amount of resisting, struggling, thinking about, or wishing they were different will change that.

It's meeting each moment with an attitude of "This is, as it is." Only from that place can you make real choices about how to respond. Later in the book we will talk about how mindful awareness and acceptance of things as they are form the ideal platform from which to take conscious action to change situations that aren't working.

Think about a situation that upset you recently. When you look at it closely, was it the situation itself that was causing you the most distress? Or was it the belief that it shouldn't be happening like that?

For example, I recall a recent time when I was taking my daughter to her best friend's birthday party (see the exercise in chapter 5). We'd left our house in plenty of time to get there, and because she hadn't had lunch, I thought I'd drive through a fast-food place to pick something up. There were several cars in line, but I assumed it would move quickly. It didn't. It took nearly twenty minutes to get through the line, and once there were cars in front and behind, there was no way to get out of the line. I accepted this as it was, and noticed my sense of annoyance, my emerging worry that we'd be late, and the little seeds of tension that were beginning to take root in my belly. No big deal.

Once we got out of the line, we got to a bridge we needed to cross to get to the party. It was a veritable parking lot. Apparently there had been an accident and lanes were closed, but they seemed to be opening up ahead. I began to have a little sense of humor about the situation—"Wow, we're really not in the flow right now." A little more tension, a little more concern about being late, but generally I accepted that these things happen. We made it through in another fifteen minutes or so, now definitely late, and made our way to the location of the party, a place I'd not been before. We entered the building, and for the life of me, I could not find the party.

At that point I was getting upset. We were about forty minutes late, my daughter really wanted to get there, and we weren't getting any closer. The mom wasn't answering her cell phone, and I started to really act up at this point—complete nonacceptance, cursing under my breath, breathing hard, very tense, hurrying from room to room asking frantically if anyone had seen the party.

Not only this, but I was also berating myself for having gotten that upset. "You're writing a book on mindful motherhood, for God's sake! How can you be so completely not accepting right now? What are you modeling for your daughter? This is terrible!"

So, what was happening for me in this situation? There was understandable frustration in response to external circumstances: a long line, a traffic jam, getting lost, my daughter's disappointment. All, for most people, unpleasant experiences. But most of my suffering, my anxiety, my tension, my worry, my agitation, my self-blame, my thrashing about mentally and emotionally came from me wanting the situation to be different and fighting against it as it was.

As it was, we got to the birthday party an hour late and had a wonderful time. And with compassion, I looked back at that journey and realized I could have made it a better experience. Sure, it was an annoying situation. But accepting the details and setting my intention to accept and move on could have made it a period of uninterrupted time with my beautiful daughter, time to tell jokes, listen to music, play twenty questions, find out more about who she is, or simply be together quietly.

Each time something like this happens, I don't see it as a failure. It's another direct experience that allows me to see more clearly. These direct experiences of what is not effective, coupled with more and more experiences of finding little bits of freedom in the midst of difficult moments, make me better and better at cultivating mindful motherhood. So, when you're tempted to think that you've "failed" at being mindful, see that as a thought and notice how experiences where mindful awareness was not present are sometimes just as useful for cultivating mindfulness as those to which you were able to bring mindful awareness.

Exercise: It Is, as It Is

Try this the next time you hit a traffic jam, during the next flight you have that is delayed, or when you're stuck in a long line. Rather than focusing on how this should not be happening, just look at the traffic jam, the delay, the line and say to yourself, "*This is happening* exactly as it is. It cannot be a different way in this moment. Perhaps, with skillful and intentional action, someday this might be different. But right now, it cannot be any other way than it is. This is just here. I'm in traffic. I'm in a long line. I'm stuck at the airport." Breathe. Notice the sensations in your body. View the situation with no resistance, no struggle, and see what happens.

Do you enjoy it now? Probably not. Do you hope it happens again soon? Unlikely. Do you find out that, deep down, you love being in traffic? I doubt it. But what *can* happen is a subtle loosening that can make a big difference. When you give up fighting the situation as it is, you might even feel your body relax, your heart open, and your mind get unstuck—as though it's been lubricated. You might begin to get creative about how to use the time. You might just practice being present, doing nothing. You might remain agitated but also be aware of that agitation, and in that awareness you may be a little less caught up in it.

The Guest House

This being human is a guest house,
Every morning a new arrival.

A joy, a depression, a meanness,
some momentary awareness comes
as an unexpected visitor.

Welcome and entertain them all!
Even if they are a crowd of sorrows,
who violently sweep your house
empty of its furniture,
still, treat each guest honorably.
He may be clearing you out
for some new delight.

The dark thought, the shame, the malice,
meet them at the door laughing, and invite them in.

Be grateful for whoever comes,
because each has been sent
as a guide from beyond.

                              —Rumi

11

the ocean of mindful awareness

let's unpack this whole acceptance thing a little further. It's hard for most people to hear the word acceptance as anything other than agreement, resignation, approval, or condoning. How can I *accept* that my baby is ill? How can I *accept* that I've been put on bed rest and my career is spiraling away from me? Why should I *accept* the criticism I get from my mother-in-law?

Acceptance doesn't mean approval or teaching yourself to somehow like uncomfortable experiences. Acceptance is not resignation or defeat, condoning or approving. It is recognition and acknowledgment on a very basic level that what is happening right now is actually what is happening right now. It's not really about what should or should not be happening but about meeting what *is* happening face to face. Acceptance is the willingness to meet each experience as it is. It is staying present and aware, even in the face of distress.

A wonderfully humorous and clear meditation teacher from the Zen tradition, Cheri Huber, puts it this way:

When I suggest we accept ourselves as we are, people get upset. The belief is that if we just accept, if we don't struggle to change, we will never be different and evil will win out over good. [I then] suggest that struggle perpetuates the "problem," and that it is really rather arrogant of us to presume that we can control something by not accepting it. Let's say I lock my keys in the car. Now, I can stomp around and curse, kick the door, and call myself names. I can do all sorts of things, but if I don't accept that my keys are indeed locked in the car, I'm not going anywhere. Acceptance doesn't mean I have to like it or approve of it or anything else. In fact, I don't have to have any relationship with it at all. I simply must accept that my keys are locked in the car. Yes, this is the reality, where do I go from here? From this place of acceptance, many possibilities become available to me that might never have done so had I persisted in my conditioned responses. (Huber 2007, 2)

acceptance is ending your argument with reality

When you argue with reality, who usually wins? Yep, reality. In fact, reality always wins. What is, actually is as it is, despite how much we want it to be not that way, or more, or less, or slightly different.

Most of our time and energy is spent trying to get things to be the way we want them to be. We do this in conscious awareness, but we also do it unconsciously. We attack a problem in our minds like a dog wrestling with a rope, pulling it this way and that. And our behaviors, especially in relationships, can become dominated by attempts to control or modify the person or situation rather than moving into each situation as it is and responding from that place.

You may say, "Wait a minute. I know someone who never tries to get things to be different—and I wish they *would* try a little harder to change things! Is that the pinnacle of acceptance?" No. Acceptance is not being passive. I'll bet if you look deeply into that person's attitudes, thinking patterns, and behaviors, even their passivity is an attempt to avoid facing things *as they are*. This is their way of struggling against reality—to ignore it or to minimize it.

Acceptance does not mean that you become robotic or complacent. It means that you see what is real and right before you and you do not resist it, deny it, or struggle against it. Acceptance is making space for whatever is going on and staying in your body while you are doing it. Far from being a passive stance, there is a warriorlike quality to acceptance.

Mindful motherhood is about creating enough space and steadiness of mind to be able to tolerate, contain, experience, and actually approach what happens between you and your child, whether pleasant or unpleasant, with curiosity and compassion. And interestingly, the full willingness to meet things as they are lays the groundwork for us to take informed and measured action to attend to things that *do* need to be changed.

I often use the word "meet" rather than "accept" because acceptance is sometimes used to mean acquiescence or even resignation. In this context, acceptance means to meet your experience, to meet the situation, as it is. To meet it as you would meet another person. To have open eyes, and in the best of times, an open heart toward whatever comes up.

Surrender is another term sometimes used to describe mindful awareness, one that carries with it equally problematic connotations. It can sound like you're being a loser or giving up. Used in this context though, surrender is the noble act of conceding defeat in your battle with what is. I prefer to think of this kind of surrender as a courageous act. Imagine it as the kind of surrender undertaken by a conscientious and kindly ruler, who, when faced with an undefeatable army, waves the white flag in order to avoid unnecessary bloodshed. Surrender is different from defeat. Surrender is seeing clearly what is and deciding to work with that.

the ocean of mindful awareness

Mindful awareness is like the ocean. There are all kinds of wild and beautiful things in the ocean, an almost infinitely variable collection of sizes, shapes, colors, of sea creatures, plants, shipwrecks, and so on. There is the sublime—dolphins playing, sea turtles soaring, whales breaching. You might see glowing umbrella jellies or majestic coral reefs. There are lots of schools of regular old tuna, hundreds upon thousands of sardines, seemingly endless. There are wide expanses of space with nothing but microscopic creatures invisible to the eye. There are a whole bunch of freaky creatures at the depths. And there are some downright ugly things under that water—sharks, stinging jellyfish, and toadfish. There are entire areas of pollution and trash. The ocean has all of these things, and "accepts" them all, without rejecting any of them. There is not the option of ejecting, avoiding, or getting away from what it does not like. The ocean itself just provides a container for all these contents.

Just like the ocean, your awareness can contain all kinds of contents, your thoughts, feelings, and sensations—some beautiful, some boring and repetitive, some downright ugly. And, you can't get rid of your thoughts, feelings, and sensations any more than the ocean can eject its contents. If you've sprained your ankle or had your car stolen, it's certainly no fun. But it's even less fun to let it ruin several weeks because you're hooked into how much you don't like that it happened. Even if you are bummed out about it, your awareness can simply let your experiences be there, just like the ocean contains its variety of contents. In fact, your awareness has *already accepted* what is happening. Otherwise, it could not be aware of it. It's typically only your thinking mind that struggles against what is.

This doesn't mean you just become passive and have no agency, no creative response, no intentional actions. You can decide to intentionally spend more time with the lovely contents of your own personal ocean. You can explore the unfamiliar contents with curiosity and get to know them better. Letting the contents of your ocean be there does not mean that you swim into a school of stinging jellyfish or volunteer yourself into the jaws of a shark. It means that you notice the shark, recognize it's there, and make a decision about how to respond to the situation as it is, rather than spending your time trying to avoid the shark, make it disappear, or wish it wasn't there.

Exercise: Accepting What Is

The next time you get upset in a small way or in a big way, check in with yourself and see if you can feel that spiral of unnecessary suffering or that tendency to make things worse creeping in. You can distinguish these states by seeing if you are chewing over the matter again and again, if thinking about it makes you harshly self-critical or critical of others, or if it just hangs on.

If you are beginning to spiral out, bring yourself into direct contact with your breathing for a few moments, focusing on the breath as it moves in and out. Home in on the space between the in-breath and out-breath, and then on the space between the out-breath and in-breath. Check in with your body's sensations, as you have learned to do, noting them one by one with just one or two words each. Come into the present moment. And then scan the situation you're facing piece by piece. Name each of its comprising elements. I am due for an event that is important to me. The babysitter is late. I'm thinking I should have called her today to confirm. I'm feeling angry at her and angry at myself. My heart is beating faster. I'm worried. Name all the pieces of your experience.

Now, one by one, intentionally and openheartedly meet each element as it is. I'm late. The babysitter is late. I'm criticizing myself. I'm angry. My body is feeling agitated. Look each element in the eye and recognize that it is happening, whether or not it *should* be. Settle into what is, in fact, happening. If you can, mobilize some compassion for yourself as you would for a good friend in a similar situation. Your words might be different, but the tone is something along the lines of, "Oh, Sweetie. It must be so stressful to be late like this." Be warm toward yourself. If you can, be warm even toward the babysitter. He or she may have run into his or her own problems or may just have made a mistake. Or maybe the babysitter was, in fact, irresponsible. Regardless of the judgment, send wishes for his or her safety and well-being.

See what happens when you approach a situation in this way. The point here is not to make yourself happy about it, or even okay with it. It's to settle into it exactly as it is and make some decisions from that place.

. . . .

nonstriving

mindful awareness has a quality of nonstriving. Not trying to make things different. Not trying to get anywhere. Not fighting or struggling. Settling down. Hanging out with things as they are for a while. Not working to achieve a goal. Not *trying* to *do* anything.

This can be confusing in some ways. You might think, "Hey, am I not *trying* to be more mindful? More aware and present?" It is a bit of a paradox. All the practice I'm encouraging you to do—even reading this book—is a reflection of your strong intention to be a mindful mom.

But, mindful awareness, more than anything, is about not trying so hard, about resting deeply in what is happening in the present moment. Mindful motherhood, as a way of being, encourages you to attend more fully to what is already present, to who you already are, to what is right in front of you, rather than striving to make things different.

In a very simple example, I recall using cloth diapers during the first three months of my daughter's life because I was concerned about reducing diaper waste in the environment. (I later learned that all the washing of cloth diapers pretty much evens out their environmental impact. Oh well!) For the first several days,

I used diaper pins to attach the diaper and always had a struggle with it. For some reason, my fingers just couldn't cram the safety pin through the folds of cotton, and I would have to refold, retry, and refold, getting more agitated each time.

Finally, one day I did a "mindful diaper change" (see chapter 18), and it changed everything. I slowed things down, paid attention to my motions, and folded the material slowly into only two layers rather than four. This way of being made putting in the diaper pin like a warm knife through butter. What changed? I stopped *trying* to change her diaper and just did it, with mindful awareness. With my awareness fully in the present moment, I saw more clearly. "Oh, a pin cannot go through four layers. The cotton needs to be thinner, so I'll try only two layers." This seems so simple, but it wasn't just a new strategy—folding the diaper differently—that helped. It was a greater peace of being that a nonstriving attitude brought. And when I think about how many times I changed diapers during those early months, and how much gentler and more nurturing each diaper change was, bringing mindful awareness to diaper changes strengthened my connection with my baby. It seems a small change, but over time, it had a pretty big impact!

Does nonstriving mean we don't take action to change situations? Absolutely not. It means that the kind of action we take is fully informed, based on our honest and forthright meeting of the situation as it is. And because our eyes are open, our actions are in line with our values and goals. When this happens we are not *trying*, not struggling to do something—we are just doing it. Remember Yoda? "Try not! Do, or do not. There is no try."

I don't want you to set up a new battle within yourself—*trying* to be mindfully aware and not be on autopilot, *striving* to be present and not be thinking about the past or the future, working hard to be nonjudging and not evaluate your experience—and then getting down on yourself when you fail.

> **Cultivating mindfulness is not about saying there is a good way to be and a bad way to be, and you now have to strive toward being the good way and not being the bad way.**

If you've read up until now, you know this idea is completely contrary to mindful awareness. But, trying to set up rules and formulas for establishing what is good and bad or right and wrong in each situation is just how the thinking mind naturally works. So, we can expect that, as the thinking mind tries to get its head around mindfulness, it sets up formulas and rules to follow, categorizes things as right and wrong and good and bad, and then attempts to solve problems.

Instead, the idea here is to *stop* trying so hard—to change things, to fix your thinking, to wrestle your emotions into being manageable, to figure things out, to line up your circumstances in the way you think they need to be in order for you to be happy. A lot of what mindfulness is is to stop working so hard. So, although mindfulness can be difficult, it's not about working hard. It's about cultivating ease. Paradoxically, this cultivation can be uncomfortable and challenging at first because it's unfamiliar. As anyone knows who has tried to learn a language as an adult, there's a period of time when it's not easy, when you are way outside of your comfort zone, and when you don't feel skilled at all.

I recall a period when I was doing research on spiritual practices and how they change people's lives. At that time I interviewed Gangaji, a spiritual teacher from the lineage of Ramana Maharshi, a well-known contemporary Hindu sage who is well-respected across many spiritual traditions for his insight and clarity of vision. I asked her, "What practice do you recommend for people who really want to grow and change?"

She paused for a moment and then replied, "Well, I would say 'stop,'" her voice emphasizing the word with the piercing authority for which she is known. "Just stop and see that what you are seeking has always been present, has always been right here."

She continued, with a twinkle in her eye. "So, I would say 'stop.' But you'll probably come back to me in a year with a book called *Stopping*, a new program on stopping, and a workshop on 'The Seven Steps to Stopping,'" she laughed (2002).

This is just how the mind works, particularly the left hemispheres of our brains, and our frontal lobes. We plan, we strategize, we judge and compare, we categorize, we come up with rules, and all of these skills are very useful for getting around in the physical world. Finding food, creating shelter, making tools, getting things done—all of these require our planning, strategizing, rule-making mind.

But those skills are almost useless when it comes to being present and con-nected, loving well, tuning in to our babies, deep listening, and so many of the things that make for being a good mom. Having healthy family interactions, fully experiencing the joyful moments, and living a deeply meaningful life depend as much on *not* striving to change anything as they do on taking skillful, intentional action when called for.

Practice Letting Go

Here are a few ways to explore the nonstriving aspect of your being:

- Take a walk and just meander, with no set time and no destination whatsoever. Putter. Follow whatever path seems most interesting at each point. See what comes up for you. If you can, set aside a whole morning or a day to do this. You might be surprised at what you encounter when you have no specific goals.

- Take five minutes to write whatever comes into your consciousness. Just write what you are aware of for five minutes. Or draw a picture of all the aspects of your experience. Toss the page when you are done. It can be interesting what comes out when you're not going to do anything with what you've created.

- The next time you clean the house, wash the dishes, or bathe the baby, get into the process rather than the outcome. Wash the dishes to wash the dishes, rather than washing the dishes to get them clean. Focus your attention on the journey, rather than the destination.

- Next time you have trouble sleeping or trouble getting the baby to sleep, take your eye off the prize. In other words, stop focusing on getting you or your baby to sleep. Sit with awakeness. Rest deeply into it. Sink into it as you would a cushy armchair. Stop trying to get anywhere. Explore what happens when you let go of any particular outcome.

13

the curious mom

another quality of mindful awareness that is really handy during pregnancy and early motherhood is something many mindfulness teachers refer to as "beginner's mind." This means approaching experiences with interest and curiosity, almost as though they were happening for the first time.

In fact, each experience we encounter *is* happening for the first time! Even if you've done a thousand diaper changes, the one you are doing now is the first time this particular diaper change has happened. Our tendency is to go on autopilot when we assess the situation and say to ourselves, "Oh, I know what this is. I've done this a million times." When driving to work along a route we've taken for years, we take advantage of the opportunity to go on autopilot so that we can—you guessed it—think, plan, ruminate, strategize, and so on.

Curiosity is examination with interest. What is this thought pattern? Why is it happening now? Wow, look at how my mind does flips around that particular person. Wow, check out that leg cramp! Oooh, when I feel guilty, my stomach gets upset. Look at this unbelievably long line. Curiosity entails approaching experiences as though they are happening for the first time, even if they may be well-worn grooves in your psyche.

comfort with the unknown

Mindful awareness is comfortable with not knowing—with uncertainty. Most of us think we should know the answers to everything, and if we don't, we should apply ourselves to figuring them out as quickly as possible. But, many of our "answers" are in fact just beliefs, stories, or "shoulds" that we have been conditioned or programmed to believe over the course of our upbringing in our families and in our society. We think that knowing the answers is a source of security and comfort, when, in fact, much of what we think causes unnecessary suffering.

As you are learning, thoughts and beliefs are not facts. They are just thoughts and beliefs—stories the mind tells us to help us understand our world. And sometimes those thoughts, stories, or beliefs are not accurate or not relevant to the current situation.

I'm reminded of an old story where a four-generation family got together for Thanksgiving dinner. Mom told her teenage daughter, "Don't forget to cut the end off the ham." The teenage daughter dutifully cut off the end of the ham before putting it in the pan and then into the oven. She thought for a moment and then asked, "Mom, why do we cut the end of the ham off?" Her mother reflected for a minute, not remembering if maybe there was a bunch of gristle at the end or whether cutting the end off allowed for better cooking somehow. Finally she said, "Hmmm, I don't actually know. Let me go out and ask your Grandma." They both went into the living room and the mother asked, "Ma, why do we always cut the end off of the ham?" Grandma looked around and said, "I don't know. Let's go ask Gigi." All three daughters asked old Gigi in her wheelchair, yelling because she couldn't hear very well, "Gigi, why do we cut the end off the ham?" "Because our pan was too short," replied Gigi.

A lot of the ways you think you should be during pregnancy and early motherhood are like cutting the end off the ham. You feel certain this is the way to do it, and certainty is a comforting state of being. When you come up against something you don't know how to do or that you don't know the answer to, you can get anxious, even angry. You can get to a place where you can't relax until you figure out or find the answer.

Becoming more comfortable with not knowing applies to all the guesses you make about other people's behavior as well. It allows you to be curious about others' behaviors, rather than assuming you know where they are coming from. This opens the door to a whole new level of communication and intimacy. When you are truly curious about them, you get to know people better, even if you thought you knew everything there was to know.

Let's say your partner rolls over and goes back to sleep after the baby cries in the middle of the night. As you sit there rocking the baby in the dark, you may stew about all the possible reasons your partner isn't with you at that moment. But, the truth is, *you are not sure* where he is coming from. You can make up a bunch of stories about his motives and assumptions, emotionally reacting to all those stories, but you don't *really* know.

Being unsure can be so uncomfortable that your mind is willing to make up pretty distressing stories about what your partner's behaviors mean, betting on the idea that the distress of that story must be better than the distress of not actually knowing. From time to time we all make premature decisions without all the information being available, just to avoid the discomfort of uncertainty. And others of us get caught in endless ambivalence, paralyzed and unable to make decisions or take action because we can't be certain of what the outcome will be.

One benefit of mindful awareness is that it is fine with not knowing. Uncertainty is no problem. Innocence, or "I don't know what the answer is," or "I am not familiar with this" becomes more acceptable. Mindful awareness recognizes that being uncertain is the most fertile ground from which creativity springs. Not knowing is the ideal platform for the emergence of innovative, new, and different solutions. Pema Chodron, the wonderful teacher in the Tibetan Buddhist tradition you met in chapter 8, says in her book *The Places That Scare You* that the essence of courage, in those situations where an old, automatic habit pattern is being triggered, is to do something different from what you would normally do (2007b).

Not knowing allows room for you to create solutions, to make decisions that are responsive to the present-moment situation, rather than relying on your habitual programming. It allows you to be more agile and nimble in the face of rapidly changing and always unique circumstances, rather than trying to fit each set of circumstances into one of your templates for "how life is." "Oh, this is one of those situations where I'm being rejected." "I've never been too good with soothing babies." "My baby is a boy, so that means he'll be more active." Mindful awareness allows you to see things as they really are, in this moment, as they are happening. It allows for that instinctual, spontaneous mothering to come through—which will lead to some of the most playful, warm, and embodied moments you'll experience as a mom.

Comfort with uncertainty also allows you to delay decisions until you have more information and to be able to tolerate the anxiety that might come along with waiting to make a decision. Being able to approach each situation with beginner's mind allows you to approach your life as if you had a wide open field of choices about what to do (which you do). You can decide how to interpret each situation you encounter independently, because you are fully present, awake, and aware and have a lot more information available to you from all your senses, not only your thinking mind. Comfort with uncertainty allows for intuitive parenting, which really just means being responsive to each situation as it arises.

Exercise: Curiosity

Curiosity is one of the most powerful forms of love and respect you can show to another person. Truly wanting to know what their perspective is, where they are coming from, what they like and don't like and why is one of the most intimate communications you can convey.

I have a good friend who always asks questions when we get together. She isn't nosy or intrusive; she's just authentically interested in everything about me during the time we are together. She asks great questions, pulling for not only my judgments or evaluations about situations and ideas, but asking exploratory questions like, "What drew you to that job?", "How did you meet your partner?", "What do you like about your daughter's preschool?", and "What do you mean? Say more…" Whenever I leave her, I find I've learned something about myself, and I feel cherished and deeply seen.

The next time you are with a friend or family member, give this level of curiosity a try. Without grilling them, just act as though you were fascinated with finding out more about them, things you don't already know and even things you think you do know. You might find you become fascinated! Now (and this may sound strange) try it with your baby—even if he or she is in your belly. For several minutes, wonder about your baby. Ask him questions. Write him a letter that starts, "I want to know everything about you…" Actively wonder. Practice curiosity.

14

cradling your experience

when you are really present, in the moment and in your body, with acceptance and nonjudgment, when you begin to cease the struggle against what is, you may notice that you automatically start to approach your experiences with greater compassion.

This is because mindful awareness is, by its very nature, compassionate. It is a gentle exploration of your experience with an attitude of friendliness. In fact, one way you can tell if you are mindfully aware when observing your experience is to see if your approach to that experience is harsh and judging or is sort of amiable. It's the difference between, "Oh heck, I do tend to get myself all twisted up around this particular issue," and "Damn it, when am I going to be able to let this go?" The first is compassionate; the second is the judging mind doing what it thinks might be helpful. Mindful awareness is never harsh and judging and usually has a flavor of compassion and friendliness.

Compassion, while it is a natural characteristic of mindful awareness, is also a process you can actively engage in. Just like mindfulness, compassion is something you may need to practice.

cultivating compassion for yourself

As a mom, you are going to make lots and lots of mistakes. Countless mistakes. So cultivating compassion for yourself, rather than the harsh self-criticism that we often think will improve our performance, is essential.

Compassion is like gently cradling your experience, whatever it may be. Even if you perceive parts of yourself as ugly, scary, small, frightened, anxious, obnoxious, or petty, hold them with the same love and care with which you would cradle your baby.

This attitude helps you recognize the pain, sadness, fear, guilt, or other forms of painful emotions that underlie some of your less desirable qualities or behaviors. You can be annoyed with yourself and not really get why you do certain things, but you can still access a deep well of self-compassion.

For example, I can think back to an experience when I was hanging out with another mom I hadn't seen in a while. The last time I'd seen her, she had a brand-new baby, was in the midst of breaking off a difficult relationship with the baby's dad, and was trying to figure out how to balance her new life as a single working mom. I felt true compassion for her, which involved not only concern for her difficulties and her grief, but also a desire to ease her suffering in ways that were realistic and empowering. I hung out with her baby while she attended a group for divorcing women, spent some evenings with her after the babes went to bed, and was available for phone conversations to be a sounding board.

A year later, after a period of time where we drifted from each other for no particular reason, we got together. She'd met a wonderful man to whom she was engaged and now lived in a gorgeous home in a desirable neighborhood. She was healthy and vibrant and clearly very happy. She was able to stay at home with her baby and was interviewing nursery schools where the baby could go three hours a day. That way, the mom could fit in some time for herself, to work out and do some writing.

My reaction? I was completely jealous. Green with envy! I imagined that I should be happy for her, and by all rights I should have been. It was so much more than I would have wished for her a year prior. But something in me lifted its ugly head, and I could only see how lucky she was. I still felt like I had to work too much, didn't have enough time to work out, didn't have enough money, wasn't feeling or looking particularly vibrant at the moment, and I was almost sick to my stomach with how much I wished for what she had in that moment.

To top it off, I got really mad at myself on the way home. What the heck was wrong with me? How could I begrudge my good friend such well-deserved happiness? Hadn't I evolved at all? What kind of friend was I? And on and on.

Then a kinder voice emerged, quietly, through all that internal chatter. Or, not so much a voice, but a sense or state of being that welcomed everything. If it had a voice, it would have said, "Of course, sweet girl, of course you want more time. Of course you want a fancy house and gym. Who doesn't? You're working so hard. How could you not? And of course you are, at your deepest and most authentic core, happy for your friend. Maybe this has more to do with arranging your life so that it is more spacious. Maybe it doesn't have to do with money at all, but with burning the candle at both ends. What can we do that will make things more nurturing and more spacious?"

As you can see, this kind of compassion toward yourself opens up room for acknowledging the truth behind sometimes confusing behaviors. When you don't act, think, or feel in ways that are in alignment with your authentic values, with the kind of mother you want to be, compassion can help you see what is underneath those responses. It encourages the younger, more wounded parts of you to come out and speak their piece, and gives you the opportunity to care for them. And it allows the more mature parts of you to craft a response that is nurturing, even toward experiences that are hard to accept.

Self-punishment, on the other hand, results in greater constriction, fear, and distress, often leaving you with a need to medicate that awful feeling with something external. That can be food, shopping, drinking alcohol, watching too much TV, or other less-adaptive forms of self-soothing. Have you ever really changed anything as a result of being mean to yourself about it? Haven't the real changes always come about as a side effect of being kinder to yourself—taking better care of yourself and your family? Have others in your life ever changed as a result of you being increasingly harsh or judgmental toward them? Hasn't a compassionate stance always been firmer ground from which to set limits with others, rather than a stance of "Let me explain to you how bad, wrong, thoughtless, and immature you are?" The same goes for you—self-flagellation results in more pain, which, in turn, results in more of the very behaviors you're angry with yourself about!

The fear is that, if we are no longer hard on ourselves, we won't do all the things we need to do. Cheri Huber, Zen teacher and author of *When You're Falling, Dive* and eighteen other great books, writes that we function under an illusion about that harsh self-critical judging voice. "The illusion is that it is on your side, that it is the voice of reason and common sense, and that to succeed at life you must listen to it" (2007, 2). In fact, she points out, through gentle nonjudging self-exploration, mindful awareness practice "allows the parts of us who have felt so threatened feel safer, and they begin to relax a little. We have created a safe place for all the aspects of who we are. Compassion has turned inward, and the joyous work of self-acceptance has begun" (2007, 4). When you feel safer, you are more effective and confident as a mom and have more room for compassion toward others. (If you're interested in reading more of Cheri's thoughts, visit www.cherihuber.com.)

Compassion for yourself doesn't mean that you never set firm, nurturing limits for yourself or that you become self-centered or self-indulgent. "Because I've had such a hard day today, I'll eat a pint of ice cream." That is not kindness to self. Even if behaviors like being chronically late, drinking too much, or overspending come from a place of underlying suffering, this does not mean they should be allowed to continue. True compassion sees the situation clearly, acknowledges the pain or grief that gives rise to the situation, and then takes realistic action to address that pain and grief. That might mean getting counseling. It might mean asking for help in other ways. It almost always means taking some action that prevents further pain and grief.

The definition of *compassion* is recognizing that suffering is present, having a strong desire and intention to reduce that suffering, and when possible, taking action to do so. This definition applies equally to others and yourself. Sometimes the strongest form of compassion is to set a nurturing limit for yourself.

At first, self-compassion takes effort. It involves thinking, acting, and even choosing to attend to different thoughts and feelings than you may normally attend to. Whereas most of us are familiar with the judging parts of our minds, characterized by thoughts like, "What was I thinking!?", "Come on, I must have made this mistake a hundred times, when am I going to learn?", and "Damn it, get a grip on yourself, girl!", it can be hard to find the more gentle, friendly voice within.

Compassion is good for you. Research by Kristin Neff at the University of Texas shows that self-compassion acts as a buffer toward negative mental and emotional states such as anxiety and depression, rumination, and thought suppression, as well as promoting positive emotional mindsets, such as greater happiness, optimism, wisdom, curiosity and exploration, personal initiative, positive emotions, autonomy, competence, and relatedness (Neff 2003a, 2003b). Like mindfulness, self-compassion is not just a form of positive thinking—cheering yourself up or reframing everything with a rosy glow. According to Dr. Neff and colleagues, "Self-compassion refers to the ability to hold difficult negative emotions in nonjudgmental awareness without having to suppress or deny negative aspects of one's experience (2008, 7)." (Sound familiar?) She continues, "Because self-compassionate individuals do not berate themselves when they fail, they are more able to learn, grow, and take on new challenges" (8). This makes self-compassion, which overlaps with mindful awareness, a great ingredient for becoming a new mom. (For more on Kristin Neff's work on self-compassion, go to www.self-compassion.com.)

. . . .

Exercise: Self-Compassion

Next time you hear that critical, judging voice berating you or being mean to you, use it as a red flag or warning signal to bring mindful awareness to your experience in that moment (in other words, just noticing and allowing it).

Your judging mind probably has its own unique voice. Discover what the tone and language of that voice is, and anytime you hear it, take it as a cue to *stop* and *breathe.* The voice may remind you of a particularly critical person in your life. It may just be mean and nasty. It may be sarcastic or sardonic (compassion and sarcasm are incompatible). It may curse or use harsh words. These signals can become really great cues for you to recognize that you've jumped on the self-judgment train of thought (which can be really hard to get off, as you may have noticed). It all starts by being aware that you are on the train.

Once you've noticed that train, use mindful awareness to watch it go by. Watch the thoughts that pass by, as though they were railcars or leaves floating along a stream. You might examine each thought as though it were a parade float, going by one by one in your parade of thinking. Note each one as it passes by. Without getting into which ones are correct and which are incorrect, just note each one as it passes.

Now see what emotions are present. Most often, when we are in judgment as opposed to compassion, the "emotions" are more like states of mind. Outrage? ("Who does he think he is?") Moral indignation? ("Unbelievable, simply unbelievable!") Martyrdom? ("After all I've done for her…") Injustice? ("It's not fair!") Recrimination? ("Why couldn't I have just…," "What's it going to take for me to…," "It was right there in front of my eyes…") Degradation? ("I'm a loser." "I'm worthless.") Hopelessness? ("I am obviously never going to get this right.")

Now look for the purer emotions underneath these states. If you find them, note them one by one. Use very short sentences to express or describe each one. "I'm feeling guilty that I was late again to pick up my babe from day care. I'm sad that I have to work and be away from my baby more than I want to. I feel grief that my mom is no longer alive to help me. I feel scared that I'll lose my old friends. I feel exhausted from taking care of three kids all day, every day."

. . . .

Look at the state-of-mind statements two paragraphs back. You may find it harder to muster compassion for those, whereas it may be easier to find compassion for the ones in the last paragraph. But as you continue to practice, you'll begin to see the earlier statements simply as signals of the later ones. As always, start with mindful awareness of your breathing, and noticing what is happening in your body. One way to distinguish states-of-mind from the emotions that lie beneath them is to know that emotions are centered in your body—especially your heart, your gut, and your throat—whereas states are centered in your mind. Judgmental or unkind statements are almost always reflections of an underlying emotion, a sadness, fear, anger, or guilt that calls for compassion rather than recrimination. When you begin to view self-critical, harsh thinking this way, you'll begin to have more compassion for yourself. In the meantime, mindfully bring attention to what lies beneath moments of judgment, rage, and the constriction or closing of your heart.

15

embodied mindful motherhood

mindful awareness does not evaluate or judge experiences or sensations as good or bad. To be sure, your mind still does and will probably continue to do so until the end of time. Mindful awareness doesn't even worry too much about that. It just notices what is present. Mindful awareness does not grasp at pleasant experiences to make them stay or try to make unpleasant experiences go away. It just sees them clearly, as they are. It meets each experience as it comes, with curiosity, gentleness, and compassion. With friendliness. At times, it examines experiences, looking at them closely, exploring their qualities, finding the middle of them and the edges of them. At other times, it allows them to flow through unexamined, simply noted and let go.

Now, if you are anything like me, you're saying, "Wait a minute. I thought she said I didn't have to become some robotic Zen mama, like nothing matters! This looks a heck of a lot like she's saying I should be some saint, some enlightened sage, who is unaffected by anything!"

All this talk about observing, being aware, noticing, or witnessing can seem to imply that somehow you'll be outside of your experience—looking down from some place on high or hovering a little bit off the ground. Nothing could be further from the truth.

Mindfulness is not avoiding, suppressing, or dissociating from your experiences. It's not detaching from your experience or working toward some robotic, unaffected tone. "Oh, look, there I am getting enraged. How utterly fascinating." Mindful motherhood is not about becoming unflappable, aloof, untouchable, or above it all. Mindful motherhood is being present, aware, and allowing of experience and remaining *in your body* all the while.

Mindful motherhood is a practice that is living, embodied, down and dirty, sensual, centered and grounded in *this* world, in *this* body, in *this* moment. It's about being present, in your body, and connected with your baby. It's playing with your baby in the dirt, rather than worrying about how it's going to get cleaned up. It's spending all morning in bed together, playing peek-a-boo, eating, napping, and cuddling, rather than having the dirty dishes in the sink call you back to work. It's allowing anger to well up as you walk your baby back and forth for the sixth time that night, or allowing yourself the shivery shudder of being sick with the flu and still having to care for your baby 24/7.

In fact, somewhat paradoxically, mindful awareness brings you into the most intimate contact there could possibly be with each of your experiences. You meet them, you greet them, and you allow yourself to move into and through them. You are aware of your experience *as you are having it*. When you are aware of being angry, you are also actually angry! You are experiencing anger. But you are also aware of it. You can see it clearly, you can experience it without making it good or bad, right or wrong, and you can express it, if you decide to.

When you are aware of thoughts like, "Why isn't my baby sleeping through the night yet?" you are actually still having those thoughts. When you're aware of feeling sad, you are still feeling sad. You are bringing mindful awareness to these thoughts and feelings *while* you are having them. And bringing mindful, non-judging awareness to them can make a big difference in how they affect your life.

In some ways, you experience everything much more fully when you are in the present moment, in your body, and aware rather than being caught up in your stories about what is happening. You begin to let each experience drench you like a warm rainfall, knowing that you cannot change it or stop it any more than you could stop the rain, and also knowing that you are absolutely capable of tolerating almost any experience you'll encounter as a mom, allowing it to arise, peak, and pass away. So don't worry about becoming an automaton through mindful awareness. It is actually a pathway to becoming more aware than you've ever been before.

diving in vs. being drowned

Most of us can get into a spiral of thought where we think about something a whole lot, chewing it over and over again. Psychologists call this kind of thinking *ruminating,* and it may sound at first like what I'm talking about—really experiencing your thoughts. But research shows that rumination is actually an attempt to *keep from feeling*—uncertainty or other emotions like fear, sadness, or anger—and that it can lead to depression and anxiety (Nolen-Hoeksema 2000). Ruminating is not mindful awareness of what is happening; it's the mind putting your experience through a meat-grinder to see if it tastes different when it's been macerated.

And if you have a tendency toward getting caught in downward emotional spirals, where you feel as though you are being sucked into a giant vortex of negative thoughts and feelings, hanging out there for long periods of time is not what I mean when I talk about allowing yourself to embody your experience. That's not diving in—it's being drowned.

Mindfulness is a way of being engaged with each experience you have with volition. You have a choice about how far into it you want to get. You have the option, if you want, to consciously examine each experience *as you are having it.* To touch into the middle of it, to look for the edges of it, to test drive it, walk around the outside of it, and kick the tires of it. Because of this, when mindful awareness is brought to positive experiences, there is an almost indescribable enhancement of your ability to enjoy and derive pleasure from them—to savor them, to milk them for all they are worth, and to let them serve as antidotes to the more difficult aspects of your life.

When an experience is distressing, uncomfortable, or downright painful, this capacity to engage with it consciously, with curiosity and compassion, makes all the difference. It doesn't necessarily take away the pain (as those of you who have been in labor know, and those of you who have not will soon find out!). It alters your relationship to the pain and allows you to actively interact with it. When you don't identify yourself *as* the thoughts, feelings, or sensations you are having, but instead are aware of them while having them, this creates space to move, to breathe. Even the smallest sliver of space around your experience can be tremendously helpful.

So while I've been recommending that you approach your thoughts and feelings, let them be there, and even be curious about them, I don't mean the kind of curiosity that killed the cat. You can learn to be aware of thoughts without being preoccupied with them. When you do get preoccupied, you can let your *mind* run along in its usual cycle, while *you* are aware of that and all the other contents of your experience. Remember, your thinking mind is only one part of who you are.

mindful awareness of your body

Bringing attention to your body and all of its sensations is a great way to come into the present moment, to come into your body, and to connect with your baby— whether still inside, still nursing or in the belly pack, or crawling all over you. In order to do this, particularly in challenging moments, you've got to spend some time getting familiar with being in your body and in the present moment, meeting things as they are without being driven to change them.

Try this embodiment meditation:

Sit in the same way you did for mindfulness of the breath, or if you won't fall asleep, lie down. Start with a few minutes of awareness of breathing.

Then, similar to the way that you brought attention gently and lightly to your breathing, bring this same quality of attention to your body's sensations. Without trying to change any of them for the moment, without evaluating any of them as good or bad (or if you are, letting that be there, too), just be aware of your body as a unified whole. Center your attention in your body. Or, said another way, allow the body and its sensations, whatever they may be, to take center stage in your awareness. Are any places in your body tight, painful, tense, or achy? Do any places in your body feel relaxed, pleasant, or have a sensation of a gentle flow or current running through them? Are any neutral, numb, or just kind of invisible—no sensation at all? You'll notice that

some body sensations are really big and noticeable, like a cramp in the leg, and others are more subtle, like the feeling of air moving across your skin. Notice them all, whether small or big.

You might try moving your attention slowly from the top of your head down through your eyes, neck, shoulders, chest, belly, arms, hips, thighs, knees, calves, ankles, and feet. Or move from feet to head systematically, simply noticing what you find in each body region. As much as possible, open your heart to whatever you find. Your thinking mind might habitually evaluate each experience as good or bad, preferable or not preferable. Just let that happen. Whatever happens is fine. The intention here is to be aware of your body, to be present in your body.

Now bring your conscious awareness into the center of your body, as though you were slipping into your body like a favorite easy chair. Sink into your body and let it hold your awareness in a warm hug. Feel gravity as it pulls your body close to the surface on which you are sitting, standing, or lying down. If you are pregnant, feel the pull of your belly, and if you are holding your baby, feel her closeness. Be intimate with the experience of being in a body.

Try this for five minutes the first time, then ten, then set a timer for twenty minutes or more.

16

present-moment mothering

now that you know that mindful motherhood happens in the here and now, in your body, not as though you were standing at some distance from your experience dispassionately, let's talk about one of the most important qualities of mindful motherhood. In fact, if I could choose only one tool you would take with you from reading this book and your mindfulness practice, it would be the capacity to *be present*.

Being present forms the foundation for mindful motherhood. It's the key to being a mindful mom. If being nonjudgmental, accepting, curious, and compassionate, and observing your experience and letting it be as it is without struggling against it are some of the rooms that make up the house of mindful motherhood, being in the present moment is the foundation of the house.

In actual fact, you are *always* in the present moment. Where else could you be? But you can probably relate to the feeling of most of your attention being focused anywhere but the present moment. There are many times when your awareness or attention is not in the present.

For example, imagine you are holding your baby and walking through your apartment because she is fussy and you want to calm her down. Your in-laws are coming for dinner that night, and your partner is at work until six o'clock. Your mind is racing, thinking about how the house needs cleaning, wondering when the baby will go down so you can clean, speculating when she'll wake up so you can go to the grocery store, and so on. Right now, it is 10 a.m., and you are in your pajamas walking through your apartment with the baby trying to get her to go to sleep, but your mind is already at dinner.

Even when you are distracted or lost in thought, you probably have mommy-radar. You are monitoring what's happening, and you'll snap out of your thoughts if the baby starts to fuss or fall over. Some part of you is always present. But this attention to the present moment is often only in your peripheral awareness. Learning to be present requires that you turn the tables so that your attention is more often on what is happening right now and your peripheral attention is monitoring everything else (like what needs to happen next, and so on).

Being present is a natural capacity. But, it's also a skill. It may not be a way of being that has been supported in you, particularly if you grew up in modern Western culture. We live in a culture of distraction, one that privileges thinking and doing over being. We are not taught to simply be present. From a very early age, sitting quietly and doing nothing may have been responded to with criticism: "Stop daydreaming," or, "Close your mouth, you'll catch flies." Sitting in silence may have led to others asking "What are you thinking?", "What are you doing?", or "Are you okay?", as though sitting quietly was cause for concern. Attitudes like these run deep and go way back—ever heard the phrase "Idle hands are the devil's playthings"? In our achievement-oriented culture, thinking and doing are seen as the best things anyone could be doing, and just sitting and being present is viewed as kind of abnormal (unless we are fully engaged in some passive activity, like watching TV).

At the same time, the results of being fully present are highly valued. We respond positively to people who have that feeling of presence. Have you ever met someone who seems like they are really there, paying full attention to you in the present moment, like for that moment there is no one else? They really listen to you with curiosity and interest, without fitting what you're saying into their previous expectations or thinking about what they will say back. They ask you questions to find out more. They are truly settled into their bodies and with you. That experience can be extremely powerful. It feels like respect, recognition, and love. Imagine being like that as a mom, knowing with gentleness and compassion that sometimes you'll get completely sidetracked but will know how to get back to being present when you become aware of it. What a gift to your baby.

You've probably experienced being fully present in the moment. Being right here, right now, with nowhere else to go and nothing else to do. Perhaps you felt it while you were in nature, or when you were playing a sport or an instrument, when you were with another person, or while engaged in an absorbing project. This kind of presence can be brought to everyday life with your baby, no matter what is happening.

you are here

So, what is being present? What does that mean? It means that you are living in real time, so that the majority of your attention is on what is happening right now. It reminds me of these old filmstrips I used to watch in history class, where a re-enactment of a historical period or event would be taking place and the booming voice of the announcer would say, "Here we are at the first Olympic games in Greece, and," the voice would thunder, *"you are there!"*

It's like that. There you are at the park, under a tree with your baby just waking up from a walk in the stroller, and *"you are there!"* Or sometimes tougher, there you are with the baby crying at 2 a.m., unable to be soothed or go to sleep, and *"you are there!"* Being here can be extremely rewarding *and* extremely challenging.

The great news for many of us is that being present with our babies can be really easy. Their adorable little selves can be incredibly compelling. You can find yourself just hanging out in the present with the baby and observing everything that is going on with great interest, curiosity, and love. In some ways this is the pinnacle of mindfulness, so it gives you the opportunity to experience it naturally without even having to try. When all the hormones line up right and you are hanging out with your baby, this experience often trumps that hypervigilance about everything else. You get "mommy brain," where everything else drops away for a while. These moments when mindfulness comes with ease are real gifts.

On the same note, when the baby is crying, it forces you to be present in ways that you may sometimes wish you could avoid, but can't. It's really hard to ignore or be distracted from your own baby crying. In some ways, these moments are also gifts. They provide a great opportunity to be present as the moment is demanding and to begin to learn how to let go into the present moment, to relax into it, to lean into it and walk right through it without all the extra suffering that comes from resisting it or trying to make it stop. The next time you're confronted with something you might typically want to get out of—a pain during pregnancy or a moment where the baby is crying—lean into it and see what happens (and try the exercise at the end of this chapter).

attention: from pinball to searchlight

Your attention can often feel like it is a pinball machine, where you don't have much choice about which direction the pinball goes—it just bounces around from place to place depending on what it rolls into. This pinball idea is actually not a bad metaphor for the contents of our experience (thoughts, feelings, sensations). They *do* sort of work like that. They are temporary, they arise and pass away, and they bounce all over the place.

But you can train your attention and awareness to be a bit more stable in the face of ever-changing experiences. When directed with intention, attention is like a searchlight. Wherever you point your searchlight becomes illuminated, and you can see what is there. When your attention, your searchlight, is not pointed at something, it is difficult to see clearly what is there. So, when your attention is not trained onto the present moment, it's hard to perceive the current situation accurately. And, in general, the more your attention and awareness is on the present moment, the more you can be responsive, awake, and creative as a person and as a mom.

For instance, when taking your baby to the playground, it can be very tempting to take the time to get on your cell phone or start texting someone you haven't contacted in a while. Even with the cutest baby in the world (yours), sometimes pushing a swing or digging in the sand is not exactly the most stimulating activity in the world. And I'm not saying you shouldn't ever make a call while you're pushing your babe on the swing.

I'm saying that if you *want* to be there, at the playground with your baby, but feel *compelled* to multitask because you're distressed by boredom, feeling worried about not getting everything done, or just can't settle down, getting used to mindful awareness in the present moment can help *you* be the one who makes the choice, rather than your thinking mind. After all, the thinking mind tends to jump around, always searching for something to think about, plan, tinker with, or *do* as soon as things get a little bit quiet. With practice in *bringing your attention to the present moment* you will be able to more often choose to be present when you want to be. You can decide to be present rather than being pulled out of the moment by whatever is most compelling in your experience.

The temptation here is going to be making this into a new rule. So, you might say to yourself, "Okay, I will not be distracted when I'm feeding the baby or when I'm at the park with him." Multitasking equals "bad mom" and being perfectly present equals "good mom." That's the thinking mind jumping in. It is the mind's habit to make up new rules and categories, and it will do this on its own. But making things black or white is not what I'm suggesting.

What I am saying is that you can choose to be present, in your body, and connected with your baby more often than not, and in those times when you *are* multitasking, you can actually be present while you are multitasking by doing the same thing. Be in the present moment. Be in your body. Stay connected. And, talk on the phone or watch TV when you need to. Just stay with yourself and your baby while you're doing it. Direct your attention to both activities simultaneously. When you stay awake and aware, you'll be able to tell whether engaging in too many activities at once is disrupting your ability to be present, embodied, and connected with your baby, and then to make choices based on that awareness.

Just bringing awareness to the fact that you are distracted and having difficulty being present or connecting is also a kind of presence. If you begin to reside more often in your awareness of what is going on, rather than being lost in whatever is going on without awareness, you'll gain a little bit of space around your experiences. And that space can be extremely freeing, offering you information and a perspective you didn't previously have.

Consider this old Zen story about a meditation teacher. He often told his students to be present with whatever it was they were doing. "When you are eating, be aware only of eating," he said. "When you are cleaning, be aware only of cleaning." "When you are meditating, be aware only of meditating." One of his students was astonished when one morning he entered his teacher's living quarters and saw his teacher eating a bowl of rice and reading the newspaper, with music playing in the background. "What are you doing?" he asked with a shocked expression. "I thought we should only do the one thing we are doing!" The teacher replied, "I am. Right now, I'm aware only of eating, reading, and listening."

What this practice is for is to give you the *choice* of where you place your attention. Eckhart Tolle is the author of *The Power of Now*, a book all about how being present in the moment can enhance your life (1999). In the book, he writes about planning for the future in the present. He recommends that if you need to plan for something, set aside some time for planning. Then, when you are in the process of planning, say to yourself something like, "Right now I am planning for the future. That is what I am doing *now*, in the present moment. I am planning for the future." Then, when you are done planning and return to having dinner with your family, *be there*, with your family, having dinner. Neither planning for the future or reflecting on the past is a problem. Living with your attention *primarily* in the future and the past (a common condition) can be limiting, and can interfere with connecting with your baby.

The focus of mindful awareness practice is to cultivate the capacity to be aware and present with whatever is happening. It is to stabilize your attention so that you can be the one who is directing the searchlight of your attention, rather than being the pinball, having your attention bounce toward whatever is most compelling at the moment.

Mindful awareness happens in the present moment. In fact, when you really think about it, everything that you can do anything about happens in the present moment. I am sitting with my baby having lunch with a friend and her baby. I am nursing my baby and reading this book. I am walking on the StairMaster, five months pregnant. In some ways, the only relevant place for your attention to be is right now, in this present moment. Motherhood happens *now*, and *now*, and *now*. As much as we spend our time focusing on the past or planning or rehearsing for the future, the only moment in which you have any power is right now.

When you are present, you can see when your baby starts to get distressed, sometimes before it turns into a full-on wail. When the baby is wailing, you can still be present with her, rooted in the present moment in your body with your breathing. You can see your baby's expressions and can better respond to what you sense your baby needs.

As you read this book, I hope that you are starting to experiment with setting aside time to practice mindful awareness (mindfulness meditation and mindful movement). I hope you also take opportunities to practice everyday mindfulness (things like eating mindfully, driving mindfully, mindful feeding and diaper changing, bringing mindful awareness to the unanticipated baby meltdown in the produce section of the grocery store). As you practice, you'll get more and more skilled at changing your attention from being a pinball in a pinball machine, bouncing around from one thing to the other without feeling like you have much choice in the matter, to being able to more often direct the searchlight of your attention where you want it to go, or at least, be more aware of where it's gone. Rather than have your attention pulled all over the place, seemingly involuntarily, you can choose to rest your attention toward what is, in fact, most important to you. But it does take some practice!

Bringing present-moment mindful awareness to activities like eating or feeding your baby can make a meal into an opportunity for connection, nourishment, and enjoyment. Driving in the present moment can be safer and can allow you time for renewal, peace and quiet, listening to music or a recorded book, or noticing things about where you live that you hadn't noticed before. Being present while breast-feeding allows you and your baby to experience a deeper connection, strengthening the bond between you. If your baby is melting down in the grocery store, you can give her your attention even if you're worried about what the other shoppers are thinking. With mindfulness, you are much more likely to respond to the situation as it is and can bring the same mindful awareness to the situation itself *and* your anxiety and embarrassment about it.

Even when you bite down on one of the fish hooks of thinking, and reflection becomes rumination or planning for the future becomes worrying about the future, you can remain present with the baby by *being aware* that you are hooked. When one of those feelings or thought patterns sticks like Velcro no matter how much awareness you bring to it, you can just let it hang there, flopping around like a fish on a hook, while you attend to yourself and your connection with your baby. When you let them be as they are, they are not really a problem.

Attention is like food. Whatever you give your attention to is nourished. If you attend to the connection between you and your baby, it is nourished. When you give attention to your thoughts, feelings, and sensations, the ones that receive the attention are strengthened. If you attend to the present moment, it is nourished. It comes alive. There is a richness and vitality in the present moment that emerges when we're not immersed only in our imaginings.

leaning into the present moment

While our natural response to an uncomfortable moment may be to think, feel, or behave in some variation of "Get me out of here!" the present-moment focus of mindful awareness helps to keep you here, and connected with your baby, even when things are uncomfortable. Being in the present moment when things are going well is equally important. This present focus can help mental and emotional well-being (both of which are linked directly to your physical well-being), your connection with your baby, and can help you moderate what is being transmitted to your baby.

So how can you get here when you recognize that your mind is elsewhere? The key is to direct the searchlight of your attention to the present moment, to the fact that you are really here, and all your thoughts about the past and the future are here, too. It's all happening right now, in this present moment. It's just a matter of getting your attention on board.

Try this mindfulness meditation:

First, bring mindful awareness to your breathing. I start nearly every mindful-awareness practice with this simple act, bringing attention to my breathing, because it is always happening in the present moment, it happens in my body, and it happens without any help from my thinking mind. Over time, when you do any of these practices repeatedly, bringing attention to breathing becomes a cue for mindful awareness because it's been linked to your practice so many times (kind of like Pavlov's dogs salivating).

So, bring your awareness to your breathing for as many breaths as it takes to feel like you can follow one breath from its beginning, when your lungs just start to draw in air, to its end, when your exhale is completely done but your inhale hasn't begun yet.

Now bring your attention to your body, as you have in other mindful-awareness practices. But this time, open your eyes and focus on a point a few feet in front of you, either in the air or on the floor. Soften the muscles around your eyes. Drop your shoulders. Use one or two words to describe what you see. Chair. Wall. Plant. Cars passing.

Bring awareness to what you hear, while still being aware of what you are seeing. Clanking glass from outside. Birds singing. The schoolyard next door. A train passing in the distance. You are seeing and hearing at the same time. Do your best to bring mindful awareness (meeting things just as they are) to all of it.

Now, while you are seeing and hearing, bring awareness simultaneously to what you are feeling in and on your body. Where it is sitting. Any aches or tensions. Warmth or cold. Air against skin. Now you are aware of seeing, hearing, and feeling. Add to your awareness any scents or tastes. Now you've got a combination—a bunch of different contents of consciousness are simmering all together in your soup pot of awareness.

You are likely thinking thoughts and are feeling some emotional tone as well. Thoughts of what you need to do later. Feelings of restlessness. Feelings of relaxation. Thought fragments swirling. Bring your thoughts, as they pass through endlessly, and your feelings, as they rise up and dissipate, into the soup pot of your awareness.

If your baby is in your belly or near you in another way, bring awareness to your baby in this present moment. Bring his current self into your awareness. You and he are here together, in this present moment.

Now, *lean into* this moment. As the Harvard professor turned meditation teacher Ram Dass says, "Be here now," with every fiber of your being (1971).

This moment, this particular stew of sensations and circumstances, has never happened before and will never happen again. There is an incredible richness to each moment when attention is brought to it in this way. So much is happening right now, it's hard to imagine needing to also include imaginings of the past or the future.

This moment is, exquisitely, exactly as it is—whether a garbage truck is pulling up outside and that's the main event at the moment or whether you are sitting with your baby on a bench overlooking the ocean. And you, your awareness, have the capacity to be present in any moment. You can choose to saturate the present moment with your attention. Join with this moment, lean into it, rest into it, and settle into it. Relax into this present moment. Feel the aliveness in your body and mind. That aliveness only happens in the present moment.

Another great exercise for being in the present moment and illuminating how much time you spend mentally in the past or the future is something you can do with a friend or partner. I got this exercise from Dave Ellis (2006), life coach and developer of the Falling Awake Program (www.fallingawake.com).

For one entire meal with a friend or partner, only talk about what is happening in the present moment. Do not talk about anything that has taken place in the past, and don't reference the past. Do not talk about anything that is coming up in the future, even later that day. It's amazing how challenging this can be!

Come Rest

Come rest here,
here in this thought,
this feeling, this moment
of great sorrow or joy.

Come rest, here in the sounds
of the children laughing
and the anguished cries
of those who imagine
they have lost their way.

Come rest here,
here in the cradle
of a warm summer night,
and the blistering cold
of winter's dawn.

Come rest in this
for there is nowhere else
to rest...

—John Astin

17

your body is a bridge to your baby

just as you are always in the present moment and it's only your attention that can swing away from it, you are also always in your body. And just as you can be distracted from the present moment, I'm sure you have times when you feel out of your body—when you feel like you're hovering somewhere nearby (probably somewhere a train of thought has taken you), but you are not really grounded right here in this body.

You've probably experienced driving to work and then not really remembering the journey there because you were on "autopilot." This is an example of living in your mind rather than your body. Or, maybe you are on a much-needed date with your partner, and you start fretting about whether you forgot to give the sitter some important information. Maybe it's that the baby can't be left on the changing table now without being strapped in because she has started rolling over, or that the babysitter needs to check the date on the frozen breastmilk before heating it, or that she shouldn't…(blah, blah, blah…). And then you end up physically on your date, but with your attention mostly at home with the sitter and the baby.

If you are an athlete or a dancer, your body may be very familiar territory. But if you're like many, you may feel that your body is primarily a vehicle for your mind—a vehicle that helps you do things like type on the computer, get from place to place, or cook dinner. If you are more like this, one of the great and challenging things about pregnancy is that it forces you to be in your body perhaps more than you're used to. When your body requires so much more attention and things that you had never given much thought to before like sleeping, tying your shoes, making love, or just getting a whole breath become acts that require all kinds of interesting acrobatics, your attention is compelled to reside more deeply in your body.

In this and so many other ways, pregnancy is a great crash-course for motherhood. For nine months, you are increasingly required to be in your body. Labor and childbirth may be the time when you are most in touch with your body—the most *embodied* any of us will ever be—though not necessarily in a very comfortable way. This doesn't end when the baby is born. Learning how to be present and grounded in your body even in the face of discomfort is a great skill to cultivate now and for the rest of your life as a mother.

centering yourself in your body

What's so great about being in your body? For one thing, your body is the primary tool through which you connect with your baby. In the first year of your child's life, your body, much more than your mind or your words, is your primary communication tool. You receive almost all the incoming information you need from your baby through your body and its sensations (as opposed to the communication we tend to focus on as adults—the exchange of ideas).

All the outgoing information you deliver to your baby goes through your body as well. You connect with your baby through your facial expressions, your warmth, your touch, your tone of voice, and your tension or relaxation in each moment. Your body is likely the primary source of nutrition, and even if you are bottle feeding, your body during feeding times nourishes your baby with important skin-to-skin contact.

Everything your baby knows about you and is learning from you during this time of ultimate brain plasticity, when neural pathways are being laid down for life, is happening through the communication between your body and your baby's body. This communication is for the most part nonconceptual—it's made up of sensations and emotions rather than ideas. It's really staggering if you stop to think about it. It's as though you've had to learn sign language rather than verbal language, but the sign language isn't just with your hands—it's with your whole body.

Because your body is so vital to your communication, paying attention to and centering your awareness in it becomes extremely important. Just like you tend to bump into things, drop things, or miss your exit on the freeway when you're distracted and out-of-body, you can be missing important incoming signals from your baby or conveying signals that you don't intend to when you are not present in your body.

Samantha's baby was crying like a howling coyote. She'd checked his diaper, had fed and burped him, and made sure there were no pinching clothes—the usual suspects. She surmised that he was tired, even though it was an hour before his usual nap time. He'd been up more than usual the night before and was doing that telltale rubbing of the eyes with the back of his hands that he did when he was headed toward sleep. Samantha was present in the moment and was perceiving accurately.

But after a while, she noticed that every muscle of her body felt tight as a violin string. Her shoulders were hunched, her movements were stiff, even her facial muscles felt tight. She realized that she'd been holding herself up rigidly, partly because she was sitting on an uncomfortable bench in the park and partly because she'd been up with the baby more than usual and was exhausted. She really wanted the baby to calm and go to sleep.

Samantha was the kind of mom who didn't like to recognize her own needs. She was a go-getter at work as a paralegal, and now, as a mom, she applied that same spirit of pluckiness to whatever came up. She enjoyed motherhood tremendously and felt like she was good at it, but she was beginning to realize that much of her strength out in the world came from her mental and psychological determination. She believed in mind over matter, willing her way through difficulties. She was rarely sick, and if she was, she prided herself on never missing work because of it. She was quick-witted, articulate, and good with ideas. All of this was a large part of her identity.

But in her new role as a mom, she was getting more in touch with her body, spending more time below her neck. As she began to include her physicality in her self-awareness, she was often surprised to find that she was wound up pretty tightly.

As her baby fussed, she found that simply bringing awareness to her body helped her begin to relax. To take it further, she pulled a blanket out of her bag, lay down with her still-crying son, placed her hand on his warm belly under his jumper, and started to breathe deeply. As she relaxed further into her body her muscles began to let go. The baby moved from wailing to creaking and then finally fell asleep, allowing Samantha to take a well-deserved nap as well.

Being present in your body means attending to your body's sensations as sources of information about where you're at and what's happening with your baby. In Samantha's case, the information was simply, "You both need to rest."

your body is a valuable source of information

Think about how it feels when you bring your entire attention to the present moment. Were you surprised by the wealth of rich data available to you? Many people are struck by how much more information is accessible when they are fully present in the moment in comparison to what is available through the filter of the thinking mind. Well, just as you gain more insight and information about the world and your experience by tuning into the present moment, focusing your awareness in your body can also yield a treasure trove of detail about what is going on for you.

Take Sally, for example. Sally was in her seventh month of pregnancy, and she spent several hours a day rubbing her bare belly and talking to her baby. The little girl inside her was a real mover and shaker and always responded to Sally's talk with long, slow stretches, flips, and kicks. One day Sally noticed that her belly hadn't grown much in the past weeks. In fact, it was looking a bit smaller. She made a mental note to talk with her midwife about it at her next visit. A couple of days later, Sally became aware that her baby wasn't responding to her when she rubbed her belly and sang. Everything seemed very still. It didn't seem right. She called her midwife immediately and they went right to the hospital. It turned out that Sally's amniotic fluid was dangerously low and her placenta was prematurely aging. The baby's heart rate was very slow, and she wasn't thriving in the womb anymore. The doctors performed an emergency C-section, and Sally's little girl was born, weighing only two pounds. (Cleo is now a strapping ten-year-old!) Sally's awareness of her body and its signals (and her taking them seriously) helped her receive information vital to the health of her child.

When you begin to pay attention to your body you will more easily hear its messages to you, whether you are getting too hot or too cold, getting dehydrated or have low blood sugar, are in need of a nap or a good night's sleep, or are right up against the edge of being sick. Your body is constantly giving you signals that tell you in great detail about your environment and your capabilities. This all may seem obvious, but it's amazing how much we ignore these basic bodily signals until they become problematic, causing changes in our mood or capacity to function. Periodic mindfulness of the body, woven throughout your day, can prevent unnecessary suffering by alerting you to elements of your physical self that need attention.

And your body is not only a source of information about itself. It can also tell you about what is happening in the present moment in your relationships with others or your surroundings. If you've ever had a "gut feeling," you know what I mean. Usually only pretty *big* gut feelings make their way into your consciousness, partly because you may not be used to consciously checking in with your body from time to time. But when you make it a habit to attend to bodily sensations as a basic part of becoming more mindful and present in any situation, you can catch more subtle sensations as well.

For example, you may have to choose a nanny, babysitter, or child-care setting at some point. Bringing mindful awareness of your body's sensations to this process can be very helpful. You can review all the references and qualifications. You can poll your friends and talk to other people who have had experience with that child-care provider. And of course you'll meet the provider(s) in person and check out the site, if it's not at your home. In addition to the facts, in which the mind is interested, take a few moments to settle into your body and see what you find during the interview or the visit. Are you tense? Is your mind telling you the situation seems great, but there is a sense of queasiness in your stomach? Does your heart feel open or closed? Do you have a sinking feeling or a feeling of comfort and security? It can even be helpful to assess the match between your body and mind. Your mind might say, "Yes, we should do this," while your body says, "No way!" Then you know it may be a decision that needs to be delayed until you become clear.

This is not to say that the information from your body is better than that of your mind. The body can feel relaxed and comfortable in situations that are simply familiar, and the familiar is not always ideal. And, as we've talked about many times now, sensations are always changing. But having this source of additional information available to you can be invaluable. If you can practice being able to access your *visceral* or body-oriented knowledge, in addition to your *conceptual* or thinking-mind knowledge, you'll be working with at least twice the amount of potentially useful information in any interaction with your baby or your world.

I am convinced that you are most skilled and authentic as a mom when your attention is in the present moment and you are in your body. This is the ideal platform from which to authentically connect with your baby and provide for his needs while setting nurturing limits. Mothering from the platform of embodiedness and presence allows you, from pregnancy all the way through early motherhood, to:

- Know that your body is a bridge to your baby

- Convey information to your baby and to others with mindful awareness (rather than being on autopilot) through your body language and touch

- Use your body as a source of information about your own state, your baby's state, and the current situation, through all your five physical senses and your intuitive sense

- Make the best decision possible with *both* your visceral, heart-and-body-centered knowledge *and* your intellectual, thinking-mind's knowledge.

Exercise: Quick Body Re-Entry

For a quick get-present-in-your-body practice that you can integrate into any part of your day, no matter where you are or what you are doing, try this exercise.

> Take a moment to sink into your body. Feel where your breathing is most noticeable—your chest, your throat, right around your nostrils? Breathe for a few moments right into that place. Now locate a place in your body that you might call the center of your being. For many people, this is somewhere along an imaginary line from your pubic bone to your heart. Center yourself in this place. Feel it become a bit weightier. Settle down into your hips. Relax deeply into your thighs. Sink into your feet. Put your body on like a glove. Take a breath and let your head settle lightly on your shoulders. Look out through your own eyes. Gently let your attention saturate your body like water soaking a sponge. Take several minutes to breathe and sink as deeply as possible into your body.

SECTION 3

Mindful Motherhood in Everyday Life

18

the dance of mindful motherhood

mindful motherhood is being present in the moment, in your body, and in connection with your baby. As I've pointed out, you are *always* actually in the moment and in your body—there is no other place to be, when you really get down to it. But it can feel like you are not. In the same way, you are always connected with your baby, whether you feel like you are or not. Bringing mindful awareness to that connection can enhance it for both you and your baby.

what is connection?

There are a few key elements of healthy connection with your baby that happen naturally, without you needing to try at all. Becoming more consciously aware of *how* you are connecting is not so much about trying to be a good mom or setting a high standard for yourself to try to achieve. Similar to mindful awareness, you can't *make* yourself connect with your baby. The connection is already there and does not need to be created. Mindful motherhood is more about being awake and aware as the connection is happening and creating the optimal conditions for the natural connection between you and your baby to emerge. For the most part, you don't need to do anything except get out of your own way and allow what is happening to be just as it is. Mindful awareness *can* help you with that.

Attunement

As a mom, having your attention in the present moment lays the groundwork for what developmental psychologist Daniel Stern called being *attuned* to your baby, or being aware of and perceiving accurately your baby's communication of her emotions and needs (1985). Attunement with your baby is sort of like a tuning fork—the baby hits a particular tone, and you resonate with that tone, reflecting it back to her with your facial expressions, tone of voice, touch, and way of being. These subtle actions communicate "Yes, I see and hear you, and I get what you're feeling." Through thousands of these little micro-interactions with your baby, her sense of self develops, as well as her own capacity to begin to learn how to deal with her emotions.

For example, let's say you're talking on the phone while the baby is playing on your lap, and the baby starts to squirm. You keep talking but begin to notice what the baby's doing. Your baby screws up her face and arches her back. Here, you could try to continue your conversation, maybe bounce the baby up and down on your knee, or toss her over your shoulder and begin to pat her back. You might tense your body up a little because you were really hoping to talk to your mom, who you hadn't talked to in several days, and you start to talk a little louder.

Alternatively, you could stop when you notice the screwed-up face and arched back, either by asking Mom to hold on for a few minutes or asking to call her back, and take a look into your baby's face and body. Naturally, you might screw your face up a little too, making a soothing sound that is the flip side of what the baby is making.

Neither of these choices is necessarily right or wrong. (I'm being serious here. It would not be mindful mothering to drop everything whenever the baby squirms). But bringing mindful awareness to this moment (being present in the moment, in your body, connected with baby, letting the experience be exactly as it is without needing to change it, and approaching it with curiosity and compassion) will help you notice what's going on in your baby's experience and make a choice about how to respond.

Attunement is not just matching your baby's state. It's making a *complementary* response, one that both conveys your empathy ("I can feel what you are feeling") and responds appropriately to what the baby is communicating. For example, if the baby gets really upset, it's not ideal attunement to get equally upset. Ideal attunement might be making sure the baby knows that you see that he's upset and reflecting a sense of being able to tolerate or contain that upset. This reaction could be holding him with firmness and making low and deep sounds. Luckily, with present-moment mindful awareness that meets experiences as they are, this comes pretty naturally—you don't have to figure it out with your thinking mind.

Use your present-moment awareness to explore what the baby may be trying to tell you. "Get me off my back. I want to be on my tummy!", "I want to sit up!", "I'm tired but can't get to sleep!", or "My diaper is wet!" You won't always be able to tell exactly what's going on, and if you guess, it will still be a story you are telling yourself about the situation. But the main thing is that you're communicating with your baby and letting her know, "I get it. I see you are uncomfortable. Let's work as a team. What can we do?"

Transmitting a secure sense of self through attunement happens in thousands of micro-interactions, not just one, or two, or even fifty. This is not about being perfectly attuned all the time—that's impossible. It's about deciding that you want to actively engage, more and more often, in present-moment awareness with your baby and cultivating the capacity to do so. Your baby is always in the present moment. Mindful awareness allows you to join her there more often.

Synchrony

A bit like attunement, *synchrony* is a way of paying attention to your baby that finds its roots in mindful awareness. You can learn your baby's "language" as it is being expressed through his movements, his breathing, his crying, and his attention—what he looks at and reaches out for, or when he turns within. Synchronous communication happens when you notice your baby's actions and engage with her in them. She sends you a signal, and you respond to it. She yelps, and you smile or jump a little or yelp back. She smiles, and you smile in return. She says "Oooh" and raises her eyebrows. You say "Oooh, oooh, oooh" and raise your eyebrows twice. This kind of repetition is baby-style play (Stern 1974). You show her with your body that you recognize her, you acknowledge her. You begin to notice what works and what doesn't by looking at the reactions you get from your actions.

As well-respected pediatricians T. Berry Brazelton and Bertrand G. Cramer (1990, 1) put it:

> As a mother learns that the rhythms of the baby underlie the capacity to attend to her, she synchronizes her own behavior to the infant's. She learns to match the infant's cues, to time her responses. She learns to turn away or to tune down when the baby does. And she learns that she can add a little bit of magnification to each behavior, which will lead the baby on. As the baby smiles, she smiles more broadly, teaching the baby how to prolong a smile. As the infant vocalizes, she adds a word or a trill, leading toward imitation. By matching her rhythms, her behaviors to the baby's, she enters the baby's world…

Mindful awareness makes all of this possible and often makes it come quite naturally. Being present and in your body allows you to become more receptive and sensitive to the baby's cues in a way that can be more difficult when you're stuck in the thinking mind.

Flexibility

Being present in your body and in connection with your baby doesn't mean being in contact, whether physically or through eye contact, all the time. It doesn't mean mirroring each and every action or matching the baby's tone exactly.

Equally, it means noticing when the baby needs to withdraw and allowing yourself to withdraw from direct contact from time to time, affording your baby the opportunity for independence in developmentally appropriate ways. You've probably experienced being next to a loved one, each of you engaged in your own pursuits, but feeling nonetheless very connected and present with one another. This kind of present, embodied connection with your baby can be just as powerful as gazing at one another.

it takes two to tango

Development in pregnancy and the first year of life is *dyadic*—in other words, it takes two to tango. You and your baby are in a dance that will determine some aspects of her long-term development. Before you feel too much pressure, there are a whole heck of a lot of other determinants that have an impact—genetics, the whole environment aside from you, and the interaction between the two. So, you can walk that razor's edge of being attuned, synchronous, flexible, awake, and aware, and you may still end up with an odd duck later in life!

Remember the balloon and the breadbox from chapter 7? The breadbox is not only the container for your experiences; it is the container for *both* your and your baby's experiences. In some ways, your job as a mom is to create the space for you and your baby to interact in ways that are optimal for his development—and yours. (It's not paid much attention, but an amazing amount of adult development or maturing as a person happens for *you* through the experience of motherhood.)

D. W. Winnicott was a pediatrician and psychoanalyst who is probably most famous for his work on "transitional objects." These are the treasured objects, like a favorite teddy bear or blankie, that help toddlers transition from relying on mom for soothing and a sense of security, to being able to regulate themselves to a certain extent (1960).

Winnicott called this breadbox-for-two the "holding environment." The *holding environment* is the whole space around and between you and your baby, physically and psychologically, as you move through your days together.

At first, you are pretty much solely responsible for creating and maintaining this holding environment. You maintain and regulate the connection between you and baby by staying present, aware, and in connection. By about three or four months old, your baby takes his turn being the leader in the dance. By this time he's contributing quite a bit to the ongoing creation and maintenance of this environment. He's eliciting facial expressions, emotions, and even thinking patterns in you. And if you've ever had your milk let down in response to your baby's cry, you know he's even driving some of your physiology.

But your job in this holding environment is to, well, *hold* what is happening. To tolerate his distressing moments, to recognize and reflect his feelings and their expressions in his body and on his face, even to be the target of and survive his anger, frustration, and aggression. You can do a kind of aikido with your baby. This is a martial art that emphasizes a reflective and complementary sparring, where you receive and reflect and give back some of what your partner throws at you, and some of it you just let pass right on through, protecting yourself by letting the force of your partner's energy fly by.

good-enough mindful motherhood

The good news is, you don't have to do all of this perfectly all the time. In fact, if you do, you'll stunt your baby's development! How's that for getting you off the perfectionism hook?

Dr. Winnicott is also well-known for his concept of the "good-enough mother" (1960). The good-enough mother begins her relationship with her baby in what Winnicott (1956) called "primary maternal preoccupation," or being basically completely obsessed with her baby (in a good way!). The mom adapts her behaviors—her thoughts, feelings, and actions—to the baby's always-changing needs, responding to each as much as possible to prevent his distress.

But over time, the mother adapts to his needs less and less, failing him in little ways that cause him manageable distress. She doesn't always get it right—bouncing him up and down and playing peek-a-boo when he wanted to wind down and withdraw into himself, or not hearing him crying in the crib after his nap while she was vacuuming.

These small misattunements, far from being problems, are what helps the baby become independent—getting used to the reality that things are not always going to go his way. When he encounters a situation where mom misses the mark, he is forced (again, in a good way) to fulfill some of his own needs. He learns to take care of himself some of the time when it comes to soothing, getting himself to sleep, and for regulating his own attention and arousal levels. So, attempting to be perfectly attuned to or satisfy every one of your baby's needs (which is impossible anyway) actually prevents your baby from developing independence. A gradual series of miniature failures are part of the normal and natural process of your baby's development. It strengthens your baby's sense of self and autonomy over time. It allows him to see you as a separate person with your own needs, and this is the beginning of your child's concern and compassion for others.

The key here is to make those failures small and age appropriate, as much as you're able. Like medicine, you give "doses" of misattunement that the baby can tolerate. I'm not talking here about deciding it's time for him to sleep through the night and letting him cry it out for hours without checking in with him from time to time. That's too much.

Winnicott would say it's *loosening* your hold a bit, but not so much so that you "drop" the baby or leave her with more emotional or physical demands than she is capable of dealing with (1967). Sometimes that happens, even with the best good-enough mother. But leaving too big a gap can often cause less independence and a less-secure sense of self in the long run. Loosening your hold is very much like mindful awareness. You learn to hold your experiences loosely, not getting hooked into them while not completely ignoring them. So as your baby gets older, you begin to notice her distress, but not react to it right away, monitoring the situation with awareness and presence, but also seeing if she can make her own way through whatever is coming up.

Mindful awareness (the capacity to be present, in the moment, in your body, connected with your baby, and meeting each experience just as it is with curiosity and compassion) can help increase your capacity to attune to your baby's needs. It can also help you to be in touch with your body and your baby's signals.

Mindful awareness can also help you better determine the difference between the optimal distress that allows your baby to learn to do some things for himself on the one hand, and when it's gone a little too far, and the demands of the situation have surpassed his developmental capacities. When you are mindfully aware, you can kind of tell when the cry is "frustrated-but-I-am-figuring-it-out-Mom," and when it accelerates to "okay-now-I'm-really-not-okay." You can begin to discern when the babe is just doing the frustrated cry and you can breathe through it and allow him to find his way. Or, you might notice when your body and feelings are shutting down, your thinking mind is inundating you with "shoulds," and the really-not-okay cry is not getting through to you.

mindfulness every day

I've outlined all the reasons why I think formal mindful awareness practice, either meditation (mindful-awareness practice while sitting quietly; chapters 2 and 3) or mindful movement (yoga, walking, or something else; chapter 4), is important. It helps you train your mindful-awareness muscle, it allows you to get more familiar with the territory of mindful awareness, and it may even change the way your brain functions.

. . . .

Exercise: The Mindful Diaper Change

There is one more way of engaging in mindful awareness practice that doesn't require setting aside time or engaging in any activity that you wouldn't already be engaging in: mindful awareness in everyday life. Different from generally taking a mindful perspective or weaving mindful awareness into your daily activities as a mom, this is intentionally engaging in a practice of bringing mindful awareness to one or more daily activities each day.

You can bring mindful awareness to any activity at all. The content does not matter. It could be writing, putting on makeup, taking a bath, being in labor, boiling eggs, cleaning the floor—anything. In this exercise, I invite you to bring mindful awareness to each diaper change.

Diaper changes are great because they can be seen as representative of the whole first year of life. They are a microcosm of your life with baby—sometimes they are fun, with baby cooing and smiling at you; sometimes baby is wiggling all over the place and you are trying to wrangle the diaper on; sometimes it's hilarious; and sometimes it just stinks. They are also frequent opportunities to connect and bond with your baby, to look into her eyes, to match your facial expression to hers, to have skin-to-skin contact, and to transmit your capacity to stay grounded in the face of discomfort, teaching her in a very direct way how to begin to deal with her own discomfort when it arises. This even applies (perhaps even more so) when you are on one of those public bathroom changing tables—the circumstances don't have to be perfect. So try this exercise the next time you change baby's diaper.

Take a moment to hold your baby against you (unless there has been a, shall we say, explosive event). Take that moment to breathe with baby. Look at her and say, "Now we're going to change your diaper," or something like that. This will signify that there is about to be a transition (from playing, or sleeping, or cuddling to being put on her back with clothes stripped off and lots of fussing around her sensitive areas).

When you lie her down, place a hand on her tummy or leg and practice mindful awareness of your connection with one another. In other words, the same way you brought mindful awareness to your breathing, to your body, or doing yoga, bring that kind of open-minded, open-hearted, present-centered, nonjudging, accepting, non-striving, curious, and compassionate attitude to this interaction. Focus on the way that you and she are in connection with one another, physically, through eye contact, and through your felt sense of being a dyad, a team, being coupled. "We two here are in this together, and I am recognizing that," is the flavor of this process.

Despite all the words I'm using to describe this, it isn't a big production. It's a few moments of mindful awareness of breathing and mindful awareness of your connection to your baby. As you strip off clothing and the used diaper, do it more slowly than you might usually. Just take your time. Even if you're in a rush, you'll find that moving more slowly is actually more efficient, resulting in less fumbling and distress. Open snaps. Pull out arm. Extract leg. Put soiled outfit to the side if necessary. There's no need to be upset, even if poop is everywhere. Remember, thinking "This shouldn't be here" is the source of more upset than it being there in the first place.

Approach it all with an attitude of friendliness, interest, and exploration. Have fun with it. Check in with your baby between each change—after removing clothes, after wiping, after replacing the new diaper. Take the time without clothing for some skin-to-skin contact, rubbing a cheek against her belly or kissing those toes.

Whether the baby is wailing and flailing or cooing and goo-gooing, it doesn't really matter to mindful awareness. This awareness just notices what's there. None of it is actually a problem when you get right down to it. Only our defining something as being a problem makes it a problem.

Take a moment after the diaper is on and clothing replaced to hold the baby to you once more. Make a humming sound, or say a deep, "Mama loves you." Help your baby revel in the relief of being dry, and mark the transition by looking at her and saying, "Now, we're done!"

· ·

A lot of being a good mom is just recognizing and being present for whatever is happening rather than resisting it, trying to change it, or pulling away. Taking a few seconds here and there to recognize transitions, acknowledge moments of relief, notice pained expressions and say something or look concerned—these are all moments of mindfulness. They say to your baby, "I'm here for you, we're in this together, and I can handle pretty much whatever you come up with." This transmits a sense of security that lays the groundwork for how your baby comes to view the world.

19

connection: it isn't always easy

being truly connected can be tough. It requires being present in the moment, in your body, and in relationship with another person (in this case your baby, though it turns out to be amazingly helpful in all your other relationships as well). Some natural connection can come easily when you are present in the moment and present in your body. Your instinctive mothering ability is given optimal conditions through which to emerge. But, a lot of things can interrupt this natural maternal instinct, and none of them are bad or wrong. Many combinations of circumstances can make it more difficult to connect with your baby from a place of presence and embodied awareness. Let's look at some of them more closely.

Your mood. Postpartum depression affects up to 18 percent of women (Gavin et al. 2005), and mild mood problems impact many more (Hopkins, Marcus, and Campbell 1984). These mood issues can interfere with your healthy connection with your baby.

Your temperament, your baby's temperament, and the compatibility between the two. Some research is now showing that some babies come into this world with an extra-sensitive temperament (Kagan et al. 1999). This means that these babies may have some difficulty being soothed, an innate need for lots of firm touch, or an innate hypersensitivity to touch and stimulation that makes it better for them to be held in a particular way, with very little touch, stroking, or caressing. Most moms are unaware of these natural variations in what babies need. Most of us have been taught that all babies need the same things, and that babies who cannot be soothed by those things are abnormal or have problems. We may have even been told that mothers who cannot soothe their babies must have some deep underlying issues. In fact, this variation is very normal, and mismatches between the mom's temperament and the baby's temperament happen all the time! But once we become more aware of these possibilities, we can face them directly rather than being lost in the stories about how it should be different.

The parenting you received as a baby or child. Due to an endless variety of circumstances, all of our parents had varying skill levels during our upbringing. Some were abusive, some addicted, some abandoning, some smothering. Some were great when we were kids but not so hot when we were babies, and some were great with some of their kids but not others. Some were mostly great but had subtle patterns that have carried through into our adult lives. Some parents were just fine, and some were nearly perfect. Some of us were adopted and some raised by grandparents. Again, none of this means that we are good or bad; none calls for shame or avoidance. It just is as it is, and in combination with many other factors, these factors can have an impact on how well we are able to connect with our babies.

Your current stress level or circumstances. You may be in a place of relative balance and well-being right now. Or, you may be having a baby in the midst of difficult life circumstances—anything from having two kids already and a partner in the military who is stationed elsewhere, to having recently lost a loved one, to having a marriage rife with conflict, or a recent divorce, or financial woes, or professional difficulties. When the level of demand in your life exceeds the level of inner and outer resources you can access, you may be especially stressed and have a more difficult time connecting.

choosing your reactions

From the perspective of mindful awareness, all of these circumstances that can impact your connection with your baby just are as they are. They are not good or bad; they are just the way things are. Wishing they were different, resisting them, ignoring or suppressing them, or trying to control them are just like trying to control your ongoing parade of experiences—limited and exhausting. Neither mindfulness nor any other approach will address all of these circumstances, certainly not in a period of the year or two you are pregnant and mothering an infant.

What mindfulness will do, however, is change the way you are aware of and respond to the circumstances you are in. You may be one of the women affected by postpartum depression, whether mild or severe. Rather than being ashamed, ignoring it, or being completely overwhelmed by it, be aware that it is a real possibility—particularly if you've been depressed in the past, but even if you haven't. If you do develop thoughts of hopelessness, worthlessness, fears of everything falling apart, something bad happening to the baby, or thoughts of harming the baby, go see a doctor and tell him or her everything.

It's like having diabetes, a heart murmur, or an ulcer. You need treatment, and mindful awareness can help you to recognize the symptoms (because the part of that is *aware* of the symptoms, no matter how small a sliver of you that is, is itself not having the symptoms). Mindfulness will also help you to accept that you have these symptoms, to ask for help, and to stay present and connected with your baby even when you don't really feel like it. There are treatments available (both medication-based and without medication), and they work.

It can be tremendously helpful to become more aware of your temperament, your baby's temperament, and the match between the two. For example, you may notice that you really love to be active—to run all over the place, have a lot of stimulation, have music playing, or maybe go to county fairs and festivals. But you may also see that your baby is totally overstimulated by any of that. Rather than forcing the issue by trying to get her to be more adaptable or depriving yourself of events that are nourishing to you, you can use mindful awareness to notice the mismatch, accept it, and come up with some creative solutions. For instance, you can go out dancing, listen to music on your headphones while you exercise, take a super-active dance class, and ask your partner or a friend to hang out with your babe. You can take your son to your favorite festival, but wrap him in a sling and put earmuffs on him.

Alternatively, you might notice that your baby is really jumpy! She actually doesn't like being caressed, cuddled, or wrapped up in a sling. She likes to be wiggling around all the time and held facing outward so she can see the world. She'd much rather be lying next to you than on your lap. You can check with a doctor, occupational therapist, or development specialist to confirm your observations if you like, and then come up with creative ways to be connected without feeling like there's something wrong with your baby or wrong with you. Using awareness, you can see *what is*, and spend your energy responding to what is, rather than focusing on the way you think it *should* be and spending your energy trying to get it to change or being upset by it.

Similarly, you can't change the parenting you received, but you *can* become aware of how your experiences as a child may impact the way you parent. As Daniel Siegel, a psychiatrist with training in pediatrics, says in the book he cowrote with Mary Hartzell, *Parenting from the Inside Out* (2004, 13):

> When we become a parent, we bring with us issues from our own past that influence the way we parent our children. Experiences that are not fully processed may create unresolved and leftover issues that influence how we react to our children. These issues can get easily triggered in the parent-child relationship. When this happens, our responses toward our children often take the form of strong emotional reactions, impulsive behaviors, distortions in our perceptions, or sensations in our bodies. These intense states of mind impair our ability to think clearly and remain flexible and affect our interactions and relationships with our children. At these times, we're not acting like the parent we want to be and are often left wondering why this role of parenting seems to "bring out the worst in us."

Mindful awareness probably won't fully process or resolve issues from your family of origin within the next few months. What it will do is make you more conscious and aware of when you are being triggered and when your current reaction seems to be overblown in comparison to the current situation (always a good sign that something from the past is being stirred up). Mindfulness will help you watch those reactions, allow them to be there, let them pass through, and allow you to make choices that are in response to the current situation rather than the past. In those moments when you do get triggered and act it out, mindful awareness can help you catch yourself more quickly and repair any damage by reinstating your mindful connection with your baby and having compassion for yourself.

I've got a good friend with whom I got a lot closer when we got pregnant around the same time and had our babies three months apart. Her challenge as a mom is anger and irritation. When she's reached her limit, she tends to raise her voice, getting frustrated and overwhelmed. While she has a daily mindfulness and yoga practice in addition to taking a small daily dose of antidepressants to address these issues, she has also accepted her innate way of being. "I'm a fiery person!" she acknowledges. So when she does lose her cool, she both reflects on the roots of that moment, using her tools to bring herself back into alignment with the kind of mom she wants to be, and she chooses not to feed thoughts that beat herself up for being who she is.

. . . .

Exercise: Quick-Connect with Baby

When you feel like you've lost contact with yourself and with your baby, try this exercise to bring you back into presence with your body and your baby.

> **Place your hand on your belly if you are pregnant, or on your baby's belly or back. Gently breathe all the way down into the base of your belly. Begin to match your breathing to the rhythm of your baby's breathing. Imagine a circle between the two of you, one being created by your dual in-breaths and out-breaths. In this exercise, you are not drawing anything from your baby nor are you transmitting anything to him. You are side by side, hand in hand, facing this world together. At times you'll lead, and at times he will. As you breathe together, you dance together, moving into the next moment.**

. . . .

20

mindful awareness
and crying

let's look at crying for a minute. When my daughter was a baby, I had the good fortune to be part of a mom's group. It wasn't anything fancy—just a group of moms gathering in the back of a baby supplies store in a strip mall on Friday mornings. But it was facilitated by a real-life baby whisperer. Marsha Podd is a registered baby nurse who provided space and good advice for a bunch of new moms, mostly with first babies, who were full of questions. (To learn more about Marsha's work, go to www.gotosleepbaby.com.)

One day, a woman whose baby was crying inconsolably finally threw up her hands and said desperately, "Why is he crying!?!" Marsha said with her typical Midwestern no-nonsense attitude, "He's just telling you he's uncomfortable."

This really stayed with me. I was often tempted to make my baby's crying into a big problem with some deeper meaning—a meaning about my baby (Sick? Colic? Spoiled rotten?) or about me (Clearly incapable? Refrigerator mother? Should be using raw milk, not goat's milk, like that article said?). But maybe crying just means, "Hey, Mom! Hey, world! I'm uncomfortable!" True, it's very loud, and it's designed by evolution to get immediate attention—yours, in particular. But crying most often is just your baby's way of talking to you. "Mom, I'm uncomfortable!"

When you bring mindful awareness to periods of crying, what happens? First, you bring attention to your own breathing—just observing it for a few breaths. Then you can quickly scan the three elements of your experience. What are the sensations in your body? Tension? Pain? Hot, warm, cool? Relaxed? What are your emotions or feelings? Fear? Exasperation? Anger? Guilt? What are your thoughts? Self-critical? Trying to think of a solution? The idea here is not to dive into any one of these realms of experience but to simply check in, notice what's happening, and breathe. Bring your attention to who you are really, the one who is aware of these three elements of experience.

Now bring mindful awareness to your baby. Just the facts. Face is red. Mouth wide open. Screaming. Fists clenched and waving, back arched. The only thing you know from his crying is that your baby is telling you in the only way he can, "Hey, Mom, something is not comfortable for me right now."

Now, free of the load of all the stories, meanings, wishing it would not be this way, and so on, you can start to *respond* rather than react. You can engage in a relatively calm process of exploration (keep breathing). Start with the things you can observe directly. Diaper wet? Hungry? Too hot? Too cold? Clothes pinching? Step by step, check each of the possibilities (and keep breathing).

If none of those things solves the problem and the baby doesn't have another truly alarming symptom, you may just need to ride it out. You can try some things, like checking for gas or a tummyache by putting some gentle pressure on the baby's tummy (either holding him jaguar style—belly down resting on the length of your forearm—or tummy down across your lap while patting his back) and reflecting on whether he burped recently. But try each possibility mindfully, as though you've got all the time in the world. Although it sounds urgent, crying usually isn't, and it can be intensified or prolonged when you get more tense and anxious. If you do tense up, with mindful awareness you can even settle into being tense and anxious.

Most often, and sometimes hardest to "diagnose," is when the baby is tired. Eighty percent of the time, your little pumpkin is just plain tuckered out. It's hard being a baby! And the process of getting to sleep is actually not so easy for many adults, much less babies, who have a lot less practice. Sometimes it's hard to leap that chasm between waking and sleeping, and crying just bridges that gap. Having mom be present, connected, and in her body helps a lot, even if the crying doesn't stop immediately.

Other possibilities for exploration have to do with soothing. You can slowly and methodically try different holds, gentle bouncing, firmer rocking, swinging, music, a warm bath—any number of things. I had great luck using a physical-therapy ball, one of those big blow-up balls that you can sit on. Bouncing with the baby while sitting on the ball, breathing, and being present soothed not only the baby, but me as well!

The key here is to focus on intentional, skillful actions rather than desperate attempts to get the crying to stop. Being creative with the crying, humming with it, chanting with it, being quiet around it, keeps you connected with your upset child. Noticing that the sound of the crying goes right through you. Feeling compassion for your baby's distress instead of focusing on getting her to stop crying lets you open to a nurturing stance. Try different things; but rather than focusing on a successful outcome (getting the baby to stop crying), make the "success" the fact that you stayed present, in your body, and connected to baby as much as possible.

Crying can last a long time, especially in *emotional-time*, where five minutes can feel like an hour. So staying connected to baby and present in your body, from moment to moment, one breath at a time, is key. You might cry. That's fine. No need to resist that either, make it a big deal, or make a story about what it means ("I'm losing it; I'm falling apart"). Sometimes the warm wash of unresisted tears is exactly what is needed for both mom and baby. After a while, explore again. See if your gut feeling, your visceral knowledge, moves you toward any gentle action.

You can also take skillful and intentional action and allow yourself to ask for help or advice. You can get this support from another mindful mom, a friendly, trustworthy person (who is not always a family member or even a close friend), or a trusted guide or pediatrician.

Having all of these options can be incredibly freeing and empowering. Surviving these trying moments while in connection with your baby forms the basis for a strong bond and a deep sense of trust, even more than the pleasant moments you share. And, through repeated experiences like this, you are actually actively transmitting to your baby his own capacity to deal with difficult moments for the rest of his life.

Notice that I say "repeated." The idea here is not that you're perfectly mindful each time your baby cries. The process is to work toward mindful awareness each time you face a difficult situation with your baby. You'll have a new opportunity to practice every time something challenging happens—and challenging things *will* keep happening, no matter how mindful you are.

21

when the going gets rough

for most people, it's easiest to be mindful (which, as you now know, just means being present, in your body, and connected to your baby, letting things be as they are, and to the extent possible, approaching your experience with curiosity and compassion) when things are going well. You might wonder why I keep repeating this definition over and over. I repeat it because, regardless of how many times I say it, the temptation is for the mind to define mindfulness as the state of pleasure, contentment, happiness, the "good" and "right" way to be. It's not. It's just being present, in your body, and meeting your experience as it is. It's a way of being that is not a state that can be "achieved," but instead is just a more effective platform from which to function in most situations.

But what about when the dirty diaper really hits the fan? When things are so difficult that it's hard to muster even a shred of sanity, much less any lofty ideal of being present, centered, and grounded? Most often, when you practice mindful awareness you find that things aren't as bad as you think—that your stories are adding unnecessary suffering to a manageable situation. But what about when the situation *is* as bad as you think, and maybe worse? What about when you are facing the worst-case scenario? Where does mindful awareness fit in then?

There was a woman in one of my groups who was just an absolute pleasure to have as a participant. Tammy was bubbly, thoughtful, cheerful, and always at the ready with a compliment or kind word for everyone. She was motivated to learn mindfulness but had trouble doing any of the practices. Each week we'd report in on how much practice we did at home, and she would say that she just couldn't get to it. Week after week she'd talk about how much she was getting out of the group but never did any of the readings or formal awareness practices. When we used one group session to focus on taking care of ourselves, she insisted there was no way she could take any time for herself because she couldn't leave the baby.

After having gently probed for weeks, we pushed a little harder for her to ask her husband for some time to herself or to hire a babysitter. Finally, with tears in her eyes, she revealed that her husband was a cocaine addict and a heavy drinker. Each day brought a new fear about whether he'd be intoxicated at home, not come home at all, or worse. There had been violence in the past and trouble with the law. But having one other young child and being a stay-at-home mom with no income or available family, Tammy felt completely trapped.

For Tammy, mindful awareness brought some internal balance in the midst of an incredibly difficult situation. "I used to literally wring my hands. I couldn't sleep. I just worried all the time and wondered where I had gone wrong, what I had done wrong," she said. "I thought he had gotten better and waited to have kids until I was sure he'd outgrown all that stuff. But now it's worse than ever. This class is the only thing that keeps me sane. I just keep breathing and doing the next thing that is right in front of me. Pay the bills? Okay. Feed the kids? Right. Go to the park. Get the kids in bed. And I am learning to keep breathing and stay in connection with my kids through it all."

Now, reading this you could say, "Wait! Tammy needs to leave the situation, to find a better solution. If mindfulness is helping her 'accept' things and stay, that's not good!" As a group facilitator, I had to consider this as well. Was mindful awareness helping Tammy stay in an unhealthy situation? I quickly concluded that if anything, Tammy's ability to remain present, grounded, and connected with her kids could only be helpful to her functioning as a mom in a less-than-ideal situation. In fact, anxiety, worry, and insomnia, while completely understandable, are not the ideal platform from which to create a healthy solution.

As much as our minds think they are helpful, chronic worry, resistance and struggle against what is happening, obsessive self-doubt and second-guessing, and putting yourself down are actually not helpful, even when a situation is really awful. Similarly, denying what is happening, suppressing your thoughts and feelings, sweeping everything under the rug, avoiding or ignoring what is happening, or justifying, rationalizing, or making excuses for it are all equally unhelpful. All those mental calisthenics are the ways we tend to deal with situations that suck.

Mindful motherhood is, once again, not happiness in the face of conflict and disruption. It's the ability to be present and remain connected with your baby, even when things are hard—sometimes even when they seem unbearable.

The experience of a close friend and colleague illustrated this to me more than anything. A psychologist and serious mindfulness practitioner for many years, Tess had a three-year-old daughter, Lucy, and was thrilled to have another one on the way. Nine months pregnant, she had scheduled a caesarean birth on the recommendation of her doctor. She gave birth to a gorgeous little girl named Sophie. One happy day passed with congratulatory visits by loved ones and Lucy meeting her new little sister. Then another day passed, and they were looking forward to going home the next day. In the wee hours of the morning, a routine check by nurses found an abnormality in Sophie's vital signs, and she was taken in for a routine screening. Tess was awakened by her husband, who looked pale and stricken. "Something's wrong…" he said shakily.

"At that moment, I somehow knew that everything in my life had changed," says Tess. "I don't know how, but I knew something was very wrong, and that this moment would be the dividing line between the time in my life when things were okay and the next part of my life. My mindfulness training told me this was only a thought, but it felt real, and in some ways, really was true."

After a false diagnosis, a harrowing ride where Sophie stopped breathing and was resuscitated in the ambulance on the way to a more intensive facility, multiple near-death crises, several open-heart surgeries, and hundreds of hours spent in the neonatal intensive care unit, Sophie was sent home. She had recovered from immediate danger but faced a series of necessary heart surgeries in the future. Today, Sophie is a gorgeous, angelic baby, in love with life and a true miracle.

Tess shared with me how mindfulness influenced her in this prolonged period of crisis:

> On the surface, there was nothing that was going to make me feel better. The pain of the situation was not going to be alleviated. This was an extended torturous experience—seven-hundred-and-fifty-million moments I had to survive, whether it was being told my baby had a 50-percent chance

*to survive, watching her go into surgery alone, being with her to have the
umpteenth catheter placed, or having it sink in that this was a lifetime illness
for which there was no real cure.*

*Mindfulness did not help me to feel better or see things differently, and
I was nowhere near "acceptance" or "nonattachment" in the general sense of
the words. What my years of mindfulness practice did do, however, was allow
me to be present to whatever was happening in each moment. No matter how
awful it was, being able to be present and connected with Sophie made it not
as bad as it could have been. Moment by moment, it was just me and her, and
when I wasn't at the hospital with Sophie, I was able to be present for Lucy at
home and give her the remainder of my attention.*

*In some ways, I didn't even consciously practice anything called
"mindfulness." I wasn't watching my breath, and I wasn't especially aware
of sensations. In other ways it was the most radical mindfulness practice of
all—simple moment-to-moment staying awake and aware, no matter what
was happening.*

*I wasn't able to point you to where my practice was. It was only in
retrospect that I can see that mindfulness training contributed to being able
to tolerate a very high degree of distress, of witnessing someone I love in
enormous pain, knowing that she might not survive. A situation like that
brings you to an instant, absolute maximum of mindfulness. The entire world
fell away—I was completely in relationship to Sophie, and to Lucy. It was like
I said to myself, "I don't care how bad it is. I'm going to be here for all of it. I
don't care if I don't think I can handle it. I'm going to be here for all of it.*

Tess related another story she'd heard from a friend about a woman who had
just finished a ten-day intensive mindfulness retreat before returning to work at
the Twin Towers in New York City on September 11, 2001. After the explosion, she
found herself in the stairwell with hundreds of other people, trying to get down
the stairs. Because of her recent mindfulness practice, she said she was able to
walk down the stairs, one by one, while so many other people were understandably frozen or attempting to race down in a big jumble of arms and legs. "It wasn't

heroic," she said. "I didn't stay relaxed. It was just step down, hand on banister, another step down, hold on, another step down…" and so on.

"I didn't feel heroic during my experience with Sophie either," said Tess. "It was just being awake and aware, moment to moment, and walking through it."

"Other things I can see in retrospect are that my mindfulness practice helped me to be very kind to the nurses, to create allies rather than spilling my frustrations out on everyone, being able to be compassionate and notice and appreciate all the kindnesses toward my family," Tess reflected. "At the same time it contributed to me being able to be strong and assertive—like telling people to wash their hands before touching her or standing up to people when they wanted to perform unnecessary medical procedures."

I asked Tess what she might tell others who were in similar crisis situations, from a mindfulness perspective. She said, with some forcefulness, "Rely on your own sense of internal authority. Inquire within yourself and identify exactly what you need in order to survive. Cut out all distractions and the things that make you feel worse. You can come back to everything later. And keep whatever helps you stay connected to yourself at all, and your kids."

Things can, and will, hit the fan in all kinds of ways. Whether a particularly hairy argument with a spouse, a car accident or injury, divorce, a serious illness or trip to the emergency room, or the death of a loved one—these are all tough situations that you *will* encounter (or ones like them). And you will benefit from bringing mindful awareness to them.

. . . .

Exercise: Losing It, Mindfully

In those internal moments where you feel like you will go crazy, want to die, want to hit someone or hurt yourself, or when you just feel like you're going to pull your hair out, there is a particular kind of mindful awareness that you can practice. This is what you can do when you are about to lose it.

First, focus on your out-breath only, giving it a little extra push as though you were blowing out a candle. Breathe in through your nose, and either blow out the imaginary candle with your mouth slightly open or with mouth closed, through the nose. Focus on the end of the out-breath.

Now bring your attention to the palms of your hands and the soles of your feet. For now, even if only for a few moments, delay drawing any conclusions or making any decisions about the situation you are in. If you are pregnant, feel your baby in your belly, the snugness with which the womb is enveloping her. Or, if your baby has been born, feel the touch of her skin against your own. If it helps to ground you, say a word or phrase that reminds you of your top priority at the moment, such as, "I am keeping myself and my baby safe," or "Be here and breathe."

In this moment, you can call on the *archetype* or universal symbol of the mother to draw upon the strength of our shared female lineage. With your mind and your heart, reach out to our ancestor mothers who, throughout millennia, have had to face unspeakable horrors and still nurture their children—keep them safe and fed, sheltered and warm. More bravely than any warrior, with more resilience than any hero (and certainly with less fanfare or appreciation), moms throughout the ages have fiercely protected themselves and their young in the most harrowing circumstances.

Now that you're a mother, you have access to this core of inner strength. Centering your attention on this resource can remind you that no one knows what they can handle until they get there. Your only job is to stay present and connected to your baby, to stay awake and see clearly. Try to do this as much as possible, moment to moment, even if you have to take it one minute at a time.

quick mindful-mama moments

Here are a few things you can do in any moment of your day, no matter what is going on, to cultivate mindful awareness:

- Find the place in your body where you can most strongly feel your breath moving in and out. Whether this is around your nostrils, in your chest, or in your belly, bring all of your awareness to this spot for ten full breaths. This brings you into your body and into the present moment.

- If you are pregnant, feel this breathing as though you can sense the oxygen in your blood moving through the placenta and into your baby. If you have an infant, hold the baby and feel the place where your breathing and your baby's breathing can be felt on your body. Focus on that place for ten breaths.

- Focus intensely on the place where the breath stops going out and starts going in, and then on the very end of the in-breath and the beginning of the out-breath. Let those two spots, those little moments when you are neither breathing in nor breathing out, be the focus of your attention for about sixty seconds.

- Bring all of your attention to the palms of your hands and the soles of your feet for ten breaths. This grounds your attention when it is flying all over the place or when you are really agitated.

The following is not traditional mindfulness. But it can be helpful if you feel as though you are too agitated to bring mindful awareness to a situation, or if you feel like your behavior might be difficult to manage:

- Find a word or phrase that is deeply calming, emotionally nourishing, or sacred to you. For some, the words "love" or "peace" are good. For millennia, people around the world have used the word "Om," which is simply the universal sound that represents the source of all that is. Even a phrase like "Be still" or "Be well" will work. Just breathe in through your nose and say this word or phrase on the out-breath, either out loud or in your mind, until your attention feels a bit more stable.

22

mindful decision making

as a mom, you are faced with all kinds of decisions, small and large, each day. What to feed your baby, whether or not and when and how to vaccinate, what day care to choose, and so on. Some decisions are easy to make, but some can be pretty tricky. Mindful awareness may not make decisions easy, but it definitely helps you to align your decisions more closely with your values and the kind of mother you want to be.

For one thing, mindful awareness brings you into contact with the many sources of information you can utilize in any situation to make a good decision. Often, we make decisions based on only one of two sources of information—we rely almost exclusively on our thinking mind, or we allow our emotions to determine what we decide. Ideally, you can also utilize some of the new capacities that you've been cultivating to make decisions.

When it's time to make a decision, use some of the muscles you've built up with your mindful awareness practices and draw upon your increasing familiarity with all the various realms of experience. Spend a few moments practicing mindful awareness of breathing. Spend a few more moments being aware of your body and your body's sensations, noting them briefly if you like with a word or two. Warm.

Tense stomach. Bloated. Relaxed. Now, attend to your thoughts on the matter. You probably have several, and some may contradict others. If you think it might help to organize these thoughts and you have time, write them down. If not, just take a moment to watch each thought go by, like leaves floating on a stream. You can take note of each one, but you don't have to pick any of them up. If you can, approach this process with curiosity, as though you were polling a number of different voices from within. Thank each one for their input. "I don't want her to go to that day care; it's not in a safe neighborhood!" Thank you; next? "I like the woman who runs the center. She's the warmest and most friendly so far." Noted, thanks. Next? Take just a few minutes (no more than five) to scan through your thoughts on the matter, touching on each one lightly, recalling that they are just thoughts, not facts.

Next, bring accepting awareness to your emotions, recalling that emotions are described by words like "fear," "sadness," "gratefulness," "guilt," "happiness," or "anger"; rather than longer phrases, which are usually thoughts masquerading as emotions. Note each emotion, one by one. And, to the extent possible, extend a sense of compassion, or at least recognition, to each one. "I'm angry about having to go back to work so soon. I don't want to have to choose a day care at all!" Gosh, totally understandable. Thank you. Next? "I'm so happy to be finding a way to have a few hours to myself." Hear, hear! Next? Survey the field of your emotions, knowing that they may contradict one another, and just touch on each one lightly, recognizing it and moving on.

Now turn your awareness to other sources of information. These are the ones that you may not often consult to make decisions. Be aware of what you can *see* about the situation, visually. "I love the cleanliness of the toys at that day-care center, but I didn't see a child gate on the steps outside." What do you hear, smell, taste, and feel? Even if these things don't seem directly relevant to the decision at hand, take a moment to note them. They can hold useful information.

Furthermore, bringing mindful awareness to the situation you are in can help you to cultivate what might be called a "mindful perspective." In other words, mindfulness may allow you access to that realm of your experience that is aware of *all* the various aspects that might hold relevant information from which to make your decision. In some ways, it's like getting a bird's-eye view on the situation, swooping in on each area of your being, one by one, to see what you find there. Only this is like a bird's-eye view from the center—of your being, your body, and the present moment.

It's good to try to strike a balance between using your gut feelings to make decisions and acknowledging the discernment of a clear mind. You can often gain more clarity when you weigh each factor equally. Consider how you think, your beliefs or stories about the situation (recalling that thoughts are not facts, and that each has varying levels of accuracy), your emotions, your body sensations, and your felt sense or gut feelings about the issue.

Then, once you've surveyed your experience for about ten minutes, sit quietly. Bring attention to breathing, to your body, and to the space in which all of these elements are arising—to awareness itself. Let go of all the thoughts, emotions, and sensations that you've just recognized, paid attention to, and duly noted. Having been acknowledged, they can now be let go. Be still. Be quiet.

I often tell the women in my classes that, in most situations, there is a part of you that knows exactly what the right answer is. But this part is often a still, small voice that requires some mental silence to be heard. It's as though many of our answers are at the bottom of a pond. Stirring the pond over and over again just stirs up all the muck and muddies the waters. When the pond is allowed to remain still for an extended period, the water clears, and the answer may become apparent.

Sometimes what becomes clear is that now is not the time to make this decision, and that it would be best to delay it. One of the most mindful comments you can make to another person is, "Can I get back to you on that?" or "Let me think about that for a minute." You can then respond after a few breaths, a few hours, or a few days. Often this interrupts your "usually scheduled programming." In other words, taking some time to reflect can help you see beyond your habitual conditioning or automatic-pilot response. It allows you to make a conscious decision, responding in the way that is best for you and your baby.

Sometimes I think back to when I was very pregnant and experiencing painful pregnancy-related carpal tunnel syndrome in my hands and arms. I was at the grocery store, and the clerk asked, "Do you want help out with that?" Even while I was thinking to myself, "Heck, it's going to be tough getting all this out to the car," I automatically said no (based on some old, rather entrenched ideas having to do with feminism and independence). I turned toward the door, and then stopped and said, "Actually, yes! Yes, I *would* like help out with these bags!" Having checked in with myself and what I really needed helped me to make a new decision, one based on what was actually going on in the present moment.

Being present, in your body, and connected to your baby can also help you stick with the decisions you've made in a way that is calm and authoritative, rather than being wishy-washy or defensive. This is partly because using mindful awareness for decision making helps you ensure that your decisions are in line with your values, your realistic capabilities, and how you want to be as a mom. Mindfulness helps you avoid making decisions simply because the decision is more familiar and comfortable, or because you've talked yourself into something because you "should" want it. Being mindful can also help you resist the temptation to make a decision prematurely because it's uncomfortable to sit with not knowing.

For example, a habitual tendency to accept every invitation out of politeness, obligation, fear of a missed opportunity, or intimacy needs might be replaced with responding according to what you and your family truly need. Mindful awareness may help you conclude that an invitation isn't right for you right now: "Actually, my daughter needs a nap, but we'd love to have a playdate later this week." In one mindful moment, you've just prevented an awkward afternoon that ends in a meltdown, rather than quality time with a friend and your baby. Mindful awareness can also help you overcome a tendency to habitually turn down help from others. You may be afraid that you'll appear needy or weak, and you may pride yourself on a sort of hyperindependence. But, when you check in with the present moment and the reality of what you and your baby need, you may be able to respond differently: "You know, it would actually be great if you could watch little Maggie while I run to the bank." Instead of operating on autopilot and old scripts that no longer serve you, taking a few breaths in mindful awareness can allow you to discern your true needs in the moment.

23

mindful eating

during pregnancy and early motherhood, eating takes on a whole new level of importance. You may be eating healthier than you used to, or perhaps eating less healthy things that you never used to. You may be eating much more than you ever have. You may be eating less, or enjoying it less, due to heartburn, reflux, or morning sickness. You might be experiencing odd cravings, like the desire for red meat, cupfuls of ice, or good old pickles and ice cream. You may be conflicted about eating because of weight gain or the desire to take weight off after childbirth. You may be enjoying eating tremendously, or you may be put off by it. Eating can become a focus of intense thought patterns, emotions, and body sensations during this time.

Bringing mindful awareness to eating can help—not only during this time, but for the rest of your life. Mindfulness can help you sense accurately what your body wants and needs. By checking in with your body, you can more accurately determine when it is hungry, thirsty, or in need of certain nutrients. Mindfulness can help you more accurately determine how full you are and when to stop eating and be satisfied instead of eating to the point of feeling overstuffed. You can sense to what extent you are resisting nourishing food because of a tendency to control food intake or eat too little, how fresh the food is, and how spicy you'd like it. All of these capacities spring from mindful awareness.

The same qualities of mindful awareness you have learned to bring to your thoughts, feelings, and sensations can be brought to the thoughts, feelings, and sensations connected to eating. Being present as you are eating, approaching whatever happens in your mind and your body with an attitude of nonjudgment, curiosity, and gentle, compassionate interest, can help you meet the changes in your relationship with food with awareness. You can accept your ravenous hunger, your revulsion toward certain smells or tastes, your anger and fear at gaining weight, your deep enjoyment of food, with compassion for yourself. No matter what is happening for you at the dining table, you can allow it to simply be present. Try cultivating beginner's mind when you eat—eating as though it were the first time.

. . . .

Exercise: Eating with Beginner's Mind

Get an orange, tangerine, or grapefruit, and try this practice. First, pretend that you are from outer space and have never seen this strange, round fruit. Hold it in your two hands, feeling the texture of the skin. Is it cool? Smooth? Pockmarked? Close your eyes and feel the fruit with your hands, noticing everything you can about it.

Bring it up to your face and feel it with your cheek. Touch it with your lips, and bring it to your nose. Inhale deeply and smell it. Use one or two words to describe what you notice, as though you were going to need to describe it to your shipmates on the UFO. Hold it up to an ear and squeeze it a little. Do you hear anything?

Now begin to peel the fruit slowly. Listen to the sound of peeling. Acknowledge how it feels as your fingers separate the skin from the flesh of the fruit. Inhale deeply again, and note how the scent changes as you peel the fruit. See what the inside looks like as you peel it.

When the peel is removed, bring it to your nose and cheek again. Rotate it in your hands. Begin to separate the sections. Continue to attend to the smell, the feel of the fruit on your hands. Notice what is happening within you. Is your mouth watering? Your stomach

growling? Your stomach turning a little bit? Any queasiness? Just let everything be there, exactly as it is. Let go of any preferences in this moment.

Now bring a section of the fruit to your lips. Take a bite. Notice what happens, both inside you and outside of you. For a moment, just note if your mind rates the experience positively or negatively. You can notice those thoughts, but try to simply engage with the experience of eating the fruit as it is. You've got nothing else to do, nowhere to go—you are fully and completely eating in this moment. Chew slowly, allowing the fruit to fill your mouth completely, noticing what you observe when you chew, when you swallow, how it feels going down your throat and esophagus, how it settles in your stomach.

Sit for a few moments with the experience of "orange" or "grape-fruit." Reflect for a moment on how it came to be in your hands, how it started from a seed, grew into a tree, ripened, was picked, and may have traveled many miles to be delivered to a market. Reflect on how many days, how much water and sunshine, how many people may have contributed to this one piece of fruit in your hands and in your mouth at this moment.

. . . .

Some people are amazed by this experience, some are annoyed, and some are bored. But most notice several new things about eating and about the fruit that they never realized before. Mindful awareness opens our eyes to a whole new world of richness and depth in the most ordinary of experiences. It can engender a level of gratitude and appreciation (both true antidepressants) for even the most mundane circumstances.

This level of mindful awareness while eating is a sort of concentration. You can try bringing this concentrated attention to a whole meal if you like. It's a very interesting experience! But it's not realistic for most of our meals.

What we can do, however, is bring mindful awareness to eating that allows for dinner-table conversation with others, simultaneous feeding of the baby, or other parts of your experience to coexist. Try this eating meditation:

Before choosing your food, take a few moments to be aware of your breathing. Then, take a few moments to be aware of all your body's sensations. Use the meditation in chapter 15, Embodied Mindful Motherhood, very briefly. Then, *choose a food in response to what you sensed in your body.* You might be surprised to find that you want only fresh fruit for lunch. You may truly want a bag of potato chips. You may desire a double cheeseburger or octopus with seaweed salad at your local Japanese restaurant. Briefly take note of any thoughts, beliefs, or "shoulds" you have about eating—and let them go. Then choose a meal that is the closest you can get to what you sensed your body wanted.

Before you start to eat, take a few breaths and look—really look—at your food. Reflect on how it came to be in your hands, quickly imagining the steps it took to get there, and sending a little bit of thanks to those who worked to bring it to you (including yourself). Settle into your body and take a bite, savoring it in your mouth with an interested, curious attitude. Consider what it tastes like, as though you've never eaten that food before (even if it is the same breakfast cereal you've eaten for years). If you need to eat quickly, then quickly savor each bite, attending to how you feel when you eat it. If you can take the time to eat slowly, do so.

When you feel only the slightest bit full, stop eating. Wait a few minutes to see if you want more. Again, notice any thoughts that arise. These might sound like, "I should just finish now," or "I might get hungry later and not have a chance to eat." Notice those thoughts with as much compassion and gentleness as you can muster, and let them pass through. Either pack up your meal for later, toss it, or have a few more bites. Sense again.

As you complete your meal, pay attention to your breathing for a few more moments, attending to whatever feelings and thoughts are present. Just note that they are there. "That felt wonderful." "I ate too much." "Yeesh, I feel sick." "Now I'm sleepy." Stay present with whatever is there, and move into the next part of your day.

the bad, the ugly—and don't forget the good!

much of this book and the Mindful Motherhood training focuses on bringing mindful awareness to difficult moments, because that is where most moms struggle the hardest. Challenges can mean that you lose connection with your baby, get distracted from the present moment and drift out of body, and behave in ways that are not in alignment with your values and goals for how you want to be as a mom.

But despite this emphasis on dealing with the tough times, bringing mindful awareness to the pleasant moments of motherhood is *equally* important. Let me say that again:

> **Bringing mindful awareness to the awe, wonder, joy, gratitude, amusement, and countless other enjoyable times between you and your baby is *just as important* as bringing mindful awareness to the difficult moments.**

I've said that sometimes it's easier to be mindful when things are going your way—when you feel at ease, you are naturally aware and present and connected with baby, and life is good. But in another way, it can be harder to bring mindful awareness to pleasurable moments.

Mindful awareness enhances motherhood not only by providing a new way to deal with difficult thinking patterns, upsetting situations, and painful feelings, but also by allowing you to bring more attention and awareness to the deep joy and satisfaction that motherhood brings. Increasing your capacity for mindful awareness enhances the quality of your motherhood in both how you engage with your baby as a mother and how you experience motherhood.

For one thing, as I've pointed out, we are hardwired to notice negative elements in our environment, both in the present moment and in our thoughts about the past and the future. Our attention is often captured by perceived threat, by what is out of place, or by what is not working. If you're already feeling down, or if you tend toward depressive thinking, it can be easier to pay attention to negative elements in your environment and to recall negative experiences than to pay attention to and recall pleasant ones. You may need to practice bringing mindful awareness to pleasant moments in the present, and you can intentionally reflect on wonderful moments in the past as well. These experiences can nourish you and serve as antidotes to the rougher times.

the squeaky wheel

Your attention is not always directed toward perceived threat or what is not working. Depending on the circumstances and on your temperament, your attention can also be compelled by whatever is the *biggest* or most intense sensation in your field of awareness, whether positive or negative. As anyone with addictive tendencies can vouch for, use of substances is not only rewarding because it helps to suppress uncomfortable feelings—it also delivers a wallop of extremely rewarding pleasure (especially in the beginning).

There can be lots of sensations in your field of awareness, but it's often the most intense ones that take up all of your attention. Often, lovely moments can get crowded out by grosser, smacked-by-a-two-by-four experiences. The delight that comes when a warm breeze blows your baby's fuzzy hair as you lean in to give her a kiss, or those first fluttering moments of the baby quickening, or that complex mix of hormonal tearful nostalgia you experience in response to a Hallmark commercial can float by almost without impact. But subtle sensations can provide richness, depth, and a certain exquisiteness to life when they are attended to.

Mindful awareness allows for greater access to these subtle realms of experience that are, in some ways, truly the spice of life. You've been encouraged to practice seeing your thoughts, feelings, and sensations as transient events, letting them move through your awareness. As you practice mindfulness more and more, you will be increasingly able to witness not only the *predominant* emotion or thought, but also the range of other experiences happening in your field of awareness at the same time, some that are even contradictory. For instance, this opening of your field of awareness can allow you to experience the pleasure of eating a perfectly ripe peach when you are hungry in a way that only pregnancy and nursing can make you, even if you have wicked leg cramps and your ankles are swollen to the size of balloons.

Mindfulness practice also increases your capacity to direct the searchlight of your attention where you choose to, rather than to what draws it most strongly. So, you can begin to choose which of your experiences you'd like to focus on or explore more in depth. Far from controlling your experience or trying to make it something it's not, this process is simply allowing yourself to move around a little in your experiences—to walk up to them, check them out, walk over to another corner, and get out your magnifying glass to look at even the little ones. You can see and feel them with a very light touch, not fixating on any one, but just examining them curiously.

Pleasant sensations, particularly if they are more subtle, can be less compelling to your attention. Therefore, you probably attend to them less. You might notice that you are relaxed, that you are enjoying yourself, that you are happy or even joyfully ecstatic. But it behooves you to actually pay attention and bring mindful awareness to those moments so that you can squeeze all the nourishing juice out of them.

Folkman and Moskowitz (2000) suggest that positive emotions are not just the polar opposite of negative ones. In fact, both positive and negative emotions run along their own continuum, from low to high, so that you can actually rate yourself highly on both positive and negative emotions at the same time! These researchers hypothesized that in people who had been diagnosed with HIV, high levels of negative emotion and stress would contribute to faster decline in health and earlier mortality. But what they found was that it didn't matter as much how much difficult emotion the people experienced—it was their capacity to experience pleasurable emotions that made the difference. People who had positive experiences in addition to their negative experiences did better than people who did not have as many pleasurable moments. So, attending to your pleasurable moments on purpose is not only about having happy feelings; it may also be good for your health.

You can bring mindful awareness to the pleasant moments of your life exactly the same way that you bring mindful awareness to the unpleasant moments. There is no difference. Mindful awareness actually does not make the distinction between happy and sad moments. It treats each with the same nonjudgmental, curious, compassionate, friendly observation. Mindful awareness is equal opportunity. It neither rejects nor elevates one experience over another. Mindfulness is a way of approaching all of our experiences with the same quality of attention, regardless of the contents of those experiences. So when those pleasurable moments happen naturally, lean into them!

. . . .

Exercise: Mindful Awareness of Lovely Moments

When something pleasant occurs while you're pregnant or with your baby, use it as a cue to bring mindful awareness to that moment. Notice your breath moving in and out. Direct attention toward your body, bringing your awareness into the center of your belly, sinking deeply into your skin—bringing your awareness into the present moment. Notice what you are seeing, what you are hearing, any touch sensations, what you are smelling, and what you are tasting. Observe what you're feeling emotionally. Without going into discursive thought or storytelling, sometimes it is helpful to note with one word each of these sensations. Warm. Relaxed. In love. Happy. Grateful. Blue eyes. Baby smell. Explore your experience with curiosity. Open your heart to what is happening right now, in the moment, in you and between you and your baby. Allow it to nourish you. And hold it lightly, for like all other experiences, it will arise, peak, and pass away.

. . . .

conclusion: mindful motherhood and beyond

mindful motherhood, above all, is a way of approaching your experiences during pregnancy and early motherhood with gentleness and friendliness. It is more and more often being in the present moment, in your body, and in nurturing connection with your baby, regardless of what is happening. It's viewing whatever is happening in your thoughts, feelings, and sensations with less judgment about whether they are right or wrong or good or bad. It's approaching the situations that make up pregnancy, childbirth, and early motherhood—the good, the bad, and the ugly—with a willingness to meet them just as they are.

This book is designed to help you spend more time in *this* moment, whether you are with your baby, at work, with your partner, or walking down the street. Even if you only practice a little bit each day, you will be developing the skill of mindful awareness—learning to observe all the sensations, thoughts, and feelings that come and go in an endlessly flowing river of experiences, both as a mother and in the rest of your life. When you practice mindful awareness, whether it is twenty minutes of awareness of breathing (chapter 2), mindful yoga (chapter 4), mindfulness of the body (chapter 15), or intentionally bringing mindful awareness to activities in your everyday life, you are spending more time *being*, in addition to thinking and doing. You are getting more familiar with the territory of mindful awareness and are increasingly able to navigate through life in a conscious and aware manner.

From this platform of presence, awareness, connection, and willingness to meet things as they are, you will find yourself more often able to respond to situations as they are rather than reacting to your stories about them or your desire for them to be different. You will increasingly make decisions and take actions that are in alignment with your values and reflect the kind of mother you want to be.

As a mom who practices mindful awareness, you'll have an increasing capacity to tolerate distress, both yours and your baby's. This expanded container for all the thoughts, feelings, and sensations you have will make it less necessary for you to compulsively engage in behaviors that are not healthy for you (overeating, overspending, overworking, raging, using substances) in order to try to deal with difficult feelings and thought patterns. You can, more and more often, let tough moments arise, take shape, peak, and pass away, just like a big wave in the ocean or a thunderstorm.

As you begin to approach your experiences with greater curiosity ("How's it going to unfold this time?"), you become more willing to try new things, depending on what the situation calls for. When you ease out of struggling with things as they are, you will free up energy to be more fully present and engaged—with yourself, with your baby, and with other people. Mindful motherhood places you right in the middle of the action, which is always right here in the present moment, and enables you to respond consciously to whatever comes up.

And as you become more aware of awareness itself, of the vast and limitless space in which all of your experiences happen, you may begin to find a sense of peace and well-being that is not dependent on circumstances. *This awareness is who you are.* You are the one who is aware of all the contents of your experience—each time you hear the baby coo or cry, each time tears well up within you, each time your heart swells with joy at the sight of your healthy, happy baby or sinks at the sight of your distressed babe, you are the one who knows all this is happening. And when you locate yourself in this knowing more and more, it can make all the difference.

As Jon Kabat-Zinn, developer of Mindfulness-Based Stress Reduction (MBSR) says:

So, in any moment, whatever is happening, we can always check and see for ourselves. Does awareness worry? Does awareness get lost in anger or greed or pain? Or does awareness brought to any moment, even the tiniest moment, simply know, and in knowing, free us? Check it out.

It is my experience that awareness gives us back to ourselves. It is the only force I know that can do so. It is the quintessence of intelligence, physical, emotional, and moral. It seems as if it needs to be conjured up but in actuality, it is here all the time, only to be discovered, embraced, settled into. This is where the refining comes in, in remembering. And then, in the letting go and the letting be, resting in, in the words of the great Japanese poet Ryokan, "just this, just this." This is what is meant by the practice of mindfulness. (2006, 4)

tending the garden of mindful motherhood

Many of the qualities I talk about in this book can be cultivated, but they do not need to be (nor *can* they be) manufactured or created. You can't make them happen. What you can do is provide the conditions that are most conducive to those ways of being.

Like growing a garden, you can't make a seedling sprout by cracking open the seed yourself, any more than you can make it grow by yanking it up through the soil. What you can do is provide nutrient-rich soil, water, and sunlight, and pull the weeds up from around the growing plant from time to time.

So, what are the nutrients, water, and sunlight you need as you grow into mindful motherhood? What makes it easier for you to be friendly toward yourself, to stop struggling against what is? What helps you to be more present in the moment, in your body, and in connection with your baby?

You don't *need* anything to cultivate mindful motherhood, but there are certainly some things that can make it easier. For example:

- Taking a little quiet time to yourself each day, or if you can't get time alone, intentionally taking quiet time with your baby or with your family

- Reading books, going to websites, or listening to talks that inspire you

- Spending time in nature, working in the garden or planting in containers, or spending time with a pet

- Having at least one friend who is gentle, kind, and a good listener but who is also honest with you and knows how to set limits

- Learning more about meditation, practicing with a group, or joining a yoga class

- Setting aside even a small space in your home to practice mindful awareness, or placing an inspirational quote, piece of art, stone, or sacred object in a small corner, your desk, or your bedside table

- Placing reminders in your environment to remind you to practice mindful awareness. Objects such as quotes, photos, or even a bracelet or necklace that you wear can remind you of your intention to cultivate mindful motherhood. Refresh or rotate these reminders every once in a while, because over time they lose their capacity to serve as cues and just become part of the background.

Now, what are the weeds, or the things in your life that reduce your capacity for mindful motherhood? Under what conditions do you tend to be harsh, critical, or judging of yourself and others? Do you need to "weed" out of your life any people or environments, or reduce your contact with them? Are your expectations for yourself so high that you are destined to fail to reach them, leaving ample opportunity for self-judgment? Have you scheduled so many activities that it takes all of your attention just to complete them all, leaving no time for simply being? Do you have distractions, habits, or compulsions that get in the way of being mindful (too much TV, substances, hoarding)? Jot down some of the things that make it hard to be mindful, such as:

- Expecting yourself to be perfect or setting unrealistic goals around meditation, diet, career, exercise, or motherhood

- Spending too much time with a critical person or judgmental people

- Chaotic environments or abusive situations

- Too many activities, leaving you no free, unstructured time

It's possible that some of these things may be out of your control. You may not be able to remove certain elements of your environment, and you may not be able to get time alone or set aside a space where you live. Don't make mindful motherhood conditional on *anything*. You can bring mindful awareness to the most chaotic or difficult circumstances and it can offer some refuge and clarity. But in those situations where you do have some influence, try to make it easier on yourself.

Finally, what are the stakes in the garden next to which the seeds of mindful motherhood can grow? What else can support you? When you honestly look at your situation (as it is, without judgment), is there any specific help you need? Do you need the help of a counselor, a pastor, a meditation teacher, or someone who has walked this path before you? Would joining a new moms' group help you? Please consider the mindfulmotherhood.org website as one of the stakes in your garden, but also seek others when necessary.

The bottom line is to be gentle with yourself. There are limitless opportunities to cultivate mindful motherhood in pregnancy, childbirth, parenting, and in the rest of your life. Much of what I've talked about in this book will come to you naturally, and more than anything, the information I've tried to convey is just a reminder to stay true to what is most real in each moment. Stay true to your center (your breathing, your body, and your connection to your baby), to that part of you that is awake, aware, and encountering each moment of motherhood for the first time. Rather than being a big project or a strenuous endeavor, mindful motherhood is about giving yourself permission to rest in this moment...and in this one...and in this one. Rest into whatever it is that is happening, and explore the adventure of motherhood with open eyes, an open mind, and an open heart.

resources

What follows are a few resources you might find helpful if you are interested in learning more about how mindfulness, present-moment awareness, or contemplative practices can enhance your well-being.

Center for Mindfulness in Medicine, Health Care, and Society
Mindfulness-based Stress Reduction (MBSR) is perhaps the most well-known secular form of mindfulness training. Available now at most major medical centers across the U.S., it takes the form of an eight-week class that meets once a week for three hours, plus a day-long retreat. To learn more, or find an MBSR class near you, go to the website.
www.umassmed.edu/cfm

Mindfulness-Based Cognitive Therapy
If you've experienced depression, you might consider mindfulness-based cognitive therapy (MBCT), which is designed to help people who suffer repeated bouts of depression and chronic unhappiness. It combines the ideas of cognitive therapy with meditative practices and attitudes based on the cultivation of mindfulness.

MBCT was developed by Zindel Segal, Mark Williams, and John Teasdale based on Jon Kabat-Zinn's Mindfulness-Based Stress Reduction program. To find a therapist trained in MBCT, go to:

www.mbct.com

Spirit Rock Meditation Center and the Insight Meditation Society

If you are interested in learning more about mindfulness meditation or in participating in a meditation retreat in which you practice mindfulness meditation with skilled teachers from one to ten days, you might look into Spirit Rock Meditation Center on the West Coast or the Insight Meditation Society in Barre, MA.

www.spiritrock.org

www.dharma.org/ims

WiseBrain.org

Go to this website for a plethora of "News and Tools for Happiness, Love, and Wisdom" at the meeting place of psychology, neuroscience, and contemplative practice.

www.wisebrain.org

A New Earth Webcast Archive

A series of ten in-depth interviews with Eckhart Tolle, author of *The Power of Now* (1999) and *A New Earth: Awakening to Your Life's Purpose* (2008). This archive also includes exercises and chat rooms and will teach you everything you ever wanted to know about present-moment awareness. Material is available for download and transcripts are available. Search "A New Earth" at:

www.oprah.com

contributors

John Astin

John Astin contributed some of the poetry in this book. He lives in northern California with his wife and daughter. Along with his work as a scientist studying the role of meditative practices in medicine and health care, he is a songwriter and recording artist and the author of *Too Intimate for Words* (2005) and *This Is Always Enough* (2007), poetic and prose reflections on the nature of nondual awareness.

www.integrativearts.com

Jnana Gowan and Powerhouse Yoga

Jnana Gowan, director of Powerhouse Education and Seminars, developed the Mindful Motherhood Yoga Series in chapter 4. Jnana conducts retreats and seminars, as well as education programs for children and adults in various arenas. Her specialty areas include: mindfulness-based prenatal yoga classes, corporate stress-reduction seminars, and wellness retreats for women. One of her favorite things in life is her preschool yoga program called Bunny Head Yoga.

www.powerhed.com

Joanne Le Cocq—Wild Rooster Productions

Joanne Le Cocq, illustrator for the Mindful Motherhood Yoga Series, is the proud mother of two wonderful boys, Frank and Evan. Joanne is a successful freelance designer and artist who works in the entertainment industry in Southern California.

www.wildroosterproductions.com

references

Astin, J. A. 1997. Stress reduction through mindfulness meditation: Effects on psychological symptomatology, sense of control, and spiritual experiences. *Psychotherapy and Psychosomatics* 66 (2): 97-106.

Begley, S. 2007. *Train Your Mind, Change Your Brain: How a New Science Reveals Our Extraordinary Potential to Transform Ourselves.* New York: Ballantine Books.

Boorstein, S. 2005. Many thanks. *Shambhala Sun*, May. http://www.shambhalasun .com/index.php?option=com_contentandtask=viewandid=2253andItemid =243 (accessed August 7, 2008).

———. 2007. *Happiness Is an Inside Job: Practicing for a Joyful Life.* New York: Ballantine Books.

Brazelton, T. B. and B. G. Cramer. 1991. The mother-baby relationship: stages in early interaction. Excerpted with permission from *The Earliest Relationship: Parents, Infants, and the Drama of Early Attachment.* Perseus Books Group, Da Capo Press: Cambridge, MA. http://life.familyeducation.com/infant/mothers/40413.html (accessed August 7, 2008).

Buss, K. A., J. R. M. Schumacher, I. Dolski, N. H. Kalin, H. H. Goldsmith, and R. J. Davidson. 2003. Right frontal brain activity, cortisol, and withdrawal behavior in 6-month-old infants. *Behavioral Neuroscience* 117 (1): 11-20.

Carlson, L. E., M. Speca, K. D. Patel, and E. Goodey. 2003. Mindfulness-based stress reduction in relation to quality of life, mood, symptoms of stress and immune parameters in breast and prostate cancer outpatients. *Psychosomatic Medicine* 65: 571-81.

Carlson, L. E., Z. Ursuliak, E. Goodey, M. Angen, and M. Speca. 2001. The effects of a mindfulness-meditation-based stress-reduction program on mood and symptoms of stress in cancer outpatients: 6-month follow-up. *Support Care Cancer* 9 (2): 112-23.

Carlson, L. E. and S. N. Garland. 2005. Impact of mindfulness-based stress reduction (MBSR) on sleep, mood, stress and fatigue symptoms in cancer outpatients. *International Journal of Behavioral Medicine* 12 (4): 278-85.

Chodron, P. 2000. *When Things Fall Apart: Heart Advice for Difficult Times.* Boston: Shambhala Publications.

———. 2003. Talking to ourselves. *Shambhala International.* http://www.shambhala.org/teachers/pema/talking.php (accessed August 7, 2008).

———. 2007a. The practice of compassion. *Shambhala International.* http://www.shambhala.org/teachers/pema/compassion.php (accessed August 7, 2008).

———. 2007b. *The Places That Scare You: A Guide to Fearlessness in Difficult Times.* Boston: Shambhala Publications.

———. 2008. *Comfortable with Uncertainty: 108 Teachings on Cultivating Fearlessness and Compassion.* Boston: Shambhala Publications.

Dass, Ram. 1971. *Be Here Now.* San Cristobal, NM: Lama Foundation.

Davidson, R. J., J. Kabat-Zinn, J. Schumacher, M. Rosenkranz, D. Muller, S. F. Santorelli, F. Urbanowski, A. Harrington, K. Bonus, and J. F. Sheridan. 2003. Alterations in brain and immune function produced by mindfulness meditation. *Psychosomatic Medicine* 65: 564-570.

Ellis, D. 2006 (May). Falling Awake. Workshop at the Institute of Noetic Sciences, Petaluma, CA.

Folkman, S. and J. T. Moskowitz. 2000. Positive affect and the other side of coping. *American Psychologist* 55: 647-54.

Gangaji. 2002. Interview by C. Vieten and T. Amorok. Video recording. November 20. San Anselmo, CA.

Gavin N. I., B. N. Gaynes, K. N. Lohr, S. Meltzer-Brody, G. Gartlehner, and T. Swinson. 2005. Perinatal depression: A systematic review of prevalence and incidence. *Obstetrics and Gynecology* 106 (5:1): 1071-83.

Grossman, P., L. Niemann, S. Schmidt, and H. Walach. 2004. Mindfulness-based stress reduction and health benefits: A meta-analysis. *Journal of Psychosomatic Research* 57: 35-43.

Hanson, R. and R. Mendius. 2007. The neurology of awakening: Using the new brain research for happiness, love, and wisdom. http://www.wisebrain.org/Wise BrainMethods.pdf (accessed August 7, 2008)

Hassan, E. 2006. Recall bias can be a threat to retrospective and prospective research designs. *The Internet Journal of Epidemiology* 3 (2).

Hopkins J., M. Marcus, and S. B. Campbell. 1984. Postpartum depression: a critical review. *Psychological Bulletin* 95: 498-515.

Huber, C. 2003. *When You're Falling, Dive: Acceptance, Freedom, and Possibility.* Murphys, CA: Keep It Simple Books.

———. 2007. There is nothing wrong with us. In *Fabric of the Future: Women Visionaries Illuminate the Path to Tomorrow*, edited by M. J. Ryan. Berkeley, CA: Conari Press. Retrieved August 7, 2008 from http://www.cherihuber.com/fabric2.html.

Kabat-Zinn, J. 1982. An outpatient program in behavioral medicine for chronic pain patients based on the practice of mindfulness meditation: Theoretical considerations and preliminary results. *General Hospital Psychiatry* 4 (1): 33-47.

———. 2006. *Coming to Our Senses: Healing Ourselves and the World Through Mindfulness.* New York: Hyperion.

Kagan, J., N. Snidman, M. Zentner, and E. Peterson. 1999. Infant temperament and anxious symptoms in school age children. *Development and Psychopathology* 11: 209-24.

Kenny, M. A. and J. M. Williams. 2007. Treatment-resistant depressed patients show a good response to mindfulness-based cognitive therapy. *Behavior Research and Therapy* 45 (3): 617-625.

Ma, S. and J. Teasdale. 2004. Mindfulness-based cognitive therapy for depression: Replication and exploration of differential relapse-prevention effects. *Journal of Consulting and Clinical Psychology* 72 (1): 31-40.

Minor, H. G., L. E. Carlson, M. J. Mackenzie, K. Zernicke, and L. Jones. 2006. Evaluation of a mindfulness-based stress reduction (MBSR) program for caregivers of children with chronic conditions. *Social Work Health Care* 43 (1): 91-109.

Neff, K. 2003a. The development and validation of a scale to measure self-compassion. *Self and Identity* 2: 223–50.

———. 2003b. Self-compassion: An alternative conceptualization of a healthy attitude toward oneself. *Self and Identity* 2: 85–102.

Neff, K., K. L. Kirkpatrick, S. S. Rude. 2008. Self-compassion and adaptive psychological functioning. *Journal of Research in Personality* 41 (1): 139-54.

Nolen-Hoeksema, S. 2000. The role of rumination in depressive disorders and mixed anxiety/depressive symptoms. *Journal of Abnormal Psychology* 109: 504-11.

Rosenzweig, S., D. K. Reibel, J. M. Greeson, G. C. Brainard, and M. Hojat. 2003. Mindfulness-based stress reduction lowers psychological distress in medical students. *Teaching and Learning in Medicine* 15 (2): 88-92.

Segal, Z., M. Williams, and J. D. Teasdale. 2002. *Mindfulness-Based Cognitive Therapy for Depression: A New Approach to Preventing Relapse*. New York: Guilford Press.

Sephton S. E., P. Salmon, I. Weissbecker, C. Ulmer, A. Floyd, K. Hoover. 2007. Mindfulness meditation alleviates depressive symptoms in women with fibromyalgia: Results of a randomized clinical trial. *Arthritis Care and Research* 57: 77-85.

Shapiro, S. L., G. E. Schwartz, and G. Bonner. 1998. Effects of mindfulness-based stress reduction on medical and premedical students. *Journal of Behavioral Medicine* 21 (6): 581-99.

Siegel, D., M. Hartzell. 2004. *Parenting from the Inside Out*. New York: Tarcher.

Speca, M., L. E. Carlson, E. Goodey, and M. Angen. 2000. A randomized, wait-list controlled clinical trial: the effect of a mindfulness meditation-based stress reduction program on mood and symptoms of stress in cancer outpatients. *Psychosomatic Medicine* 62 (5): 613-22.

Stern, D. 1974. The goal and structure of mother-infant play. *Journal of the American Academy of Child Psychiatry* 13: 402-21.

———. 1985. *The Interpersonal World of the Infant*. New York: Basic Books.

Teasdale, J. D., Z. V. Segal, J. M. Williams, V. A. Ridgeway, J. M. Soulsby, and M. A. Lau. 2000. Prevention of relapse/recurrence in major depression by mindfulness-based cognitive therapy. *Journal of Consulting and Clinical Psychology* 68 (4): 615-23.

Teasdale, J., R. Moore, H. Hayhurst, M. Pope, S. Williams, and Z. V. Segal. 2002. Metacognitive awareness and prevention of relapse in depression: Empirical evidence. *Journal of Consulting and Clinical Psychology* 70 (2): 275-87.

Tolle, E. 1999. *The Power of Now: A Guide to Spiritual Enlightenment*. Novato, CA: New World Library.

Vieten, C. and J. Astin. 2008. Effects of a mindfulness-based intervention during pregnancy: Results of a pilot study. *Archives of Women's Mental Health* 11: 67-74.

Winnicott, D. 1956. *Collected Papers: Through Paediatrics to Psychoanalysis*. London: Hogarth.

———. 1960. The theory of the parent-child relationship. *International Journal of Psychoanalysis* 41: 585-595.

———. 1967. Mirror-role of the mother and family in child development. In *The Predicament of the Family: A Psycho-Analytical Symposium,* edited P. Lomas. London: Hogarth.

Photo by W. Jo Moser
Photography

Cassandra Vieten, Ph.D., is a licensed clinical psychologist, director of research at the Institute of Noetic Sciences, codirector of the Mind Body Medicine Research Group at California Pacific Medical Center Research Institute in San Francisco, CA, and copresident of the Institute for Spirituality and Psychology. Her research has focused on mindfulness-based approaches to cultivating emotional balance, the involvement of biology, psychology, and emotion in addiction and recovery, the role of compassionate intent and belief in healing, and the factors, experiences, and practices involved in psychospiritual transformation. She has published several academic articles and chapters, has conducted numerous presentations at international scientific conferences, and is coauthor of *Living Deeply*.

Foreword writer **Sylvia Boorstein, Ph.D.**, is a founding teacher of Spirit Rock Meditation Center and a psychotherapist, wife, mother, and grandmother. She is author of several books, including *It's Easier Than You Think* and *Happiness Is an Inside Job*.

About the Institute of Noetic Sciences (IONS)

Noetic Books is an imprint of the Institute of Noetic Sciences, which was founded in 1973 by Apollo 14 astronaut Edgar Mitchell. IONS is a 501(c)(3) nonprofit research, education, and membership organization whose mission is advancing the science of consciousness and human experience to serve individual and collective transformation. "Noetic" comes from the Greek word *nous*, which means "intuitive mind" or "inner knowing." The Institute's primary program areas include consciousness and healing, extended human capacities, and emerging worldviews. The specific work of the institute includes the following:

- Sponsorship of and participation in original research

- Publication of the quarterly magazine *Shift: At the Frontiers of Consciousness*

- The monthly membership program, Shift in Action, and its associated website, www.shiftinaction.com

- Presentation and cosponsorship of regional and international workshops and conferences

- The hosting of residential seminars and workshops at its on-campus retreat facility, located on 200 acres thirty minutes north of San Francisco

- The support of a global volunteer network of community groups

IONS also publishes *The Shift Report*, a now bi-annual publication that charts shifts in worldview across a wide range of disciplines and areas of human activity. Information on these reports can be found at *www.shiftreport.org*. More information about Noetic Books is available at *www.noeticbooks.org*.

To learn more about the Institute and its activities and programs, please contact

Institute of Noetic Sciences
101 San Antonio Road
Petaluma, CA 94952-9524
707-775-3500 / fax: 707-781-7420
www.noetic.org

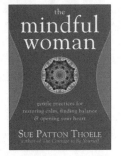

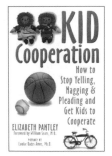
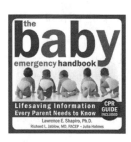